Be Careful What You Call

IMPOSSIBLE

JOHN HAGGAI

HARVEST HOUSE PUBLISHERS
Eugene, Oregon 97402

BE CAREFUL WHAT YOU CALL IMPOSSIBLE

Copyright © 1989 by John Haggai
Published by Harvest House Publishers
Eugene, Oregon 97402

Library of Congress Cataloging-in-Publication Data

Haggai, John Edmund.
    Be careful what you call impossible / John Haggai.
    1. Success—Religious aspects—Christianity.   2. Goal (Psychology).   I. Title.
BV4598.3.H34   1989   89-31533
158'.1—dc20   CIP
ISBN 0-89081-745-9

Printed in the United States of America.

ACKNOWLEDGMENTS

I wrote this book because Bob Hawkins, Sr., of Harvest House asked me to. The moment he mentioned it, the light went on in my head. I knew his request was valid; the book was necessary.

I'm indebted to scores of people who, at my request, sent me their experiences of turning the impossible into the possible. Unfortunately, I could not use all of the stories, or the book would have turned out to be unmanageably large. However, in a subsequent volume, I intend to include the unused stories that were eliminated in this edition.

David Lee of Edinburgh, Scotland, helped me enormously. It seems as though he can crawl inside my head, read my thought processes, and give form and shape to my convictions.

Norma Byrd, my literary assistant, has been of invaluable assistance, and I would be remiss if I didn't thank John McCollister, my instructor in writing, for giving the book the benefit of his editorial eye.

CONTENTS

PREFACE

It has for years troubled me that some people face life's challenges with the exclusive response, "I'm waiting on the Lord." They do nothing. They give up easily. When things don't work out well, they immediately blame circumstances. I like what 19th-century American evangelist Dwight L. Moody said, "It's fine to wait on the Lord as long as you're hustling while you're waiting."

On the other hand, there are people who make no reference of their experiences to the Lord. They try to go it alone. They try to do it in their own strength. And that is even more tragic.

James, the author of the book bearing his name in the Bible's New Testament, talked about faith and works:

> Faith by itself, if it does not have works, is dead. . . . Show me your faith without your work, and I will show you my faith by my works (James 2:17,18).

I'm praying that this book will encourage people to reference every facet of their lives to the will of God. I want it to show a way out to those who feel boxed in by seeming impossibilities. I am also hoping those who refuse to organize and persist for a desired conclusion—perhaps through misunderstanding or even laziness—will come to know that God does not do for us what He has enabled us to do for ourselves.

In 1988, I published a book entitled *The Leading Edge* (Word Books, Waco, Texas). If you want an illustration of the "Impossible to Possible" theme in terms of one's vocation, you will find this entire book to be an example of what I'm writing in this volume.

Certain things, of course, will always be impossible. I have a bass voice. There's no possibility of my becoming a Metropolitan coloratura soprano. I am 5 feet 7½ inches tall and have passed my 65th birthday. There is no possibility that I'm going to be the center for the Boston Celtics.

Nevertheless, there are so many areas of our lives that need to be corrected by a new trust, a new discipline in organization, and a new steadfastness in persistence.

To that end I have presented the TOP principles (TRUST, ORGANIZE, PERSIST) with the hope that many who are floundering will find purpose and pursue it.

To the spirit of
Waddy Abraham Haggai
within each one of us
waiting to be awakened

1

A Fresh Start

The sound of a siren is so common in a big city that few heads turned one November morning in Chicago as an ambulance wailed and flashed through a busy intersection. Moments earlier a maid had discovered an empty pill bottle and the inert body of a young woman in an exclusive hotel room.

Heather Carmichael was rushed to the hospital.

During the noon meal that fateful day, Heather's parents received the phone call relating the devastating news. Filled with horror and disbelief, they drove to the hospital to find the emergency doctor attending her.

"What are her chances?" they asked.

"I can't say. But I'll tell you—you have a mess on your hands."

He left them to wait and pray in an agony of doubt for two whole days.

Heather regained consciousness, aware of the tubes in her throat and arms. "I'm alive," she thought. But life seemed like a distant, dim shaft of light falling through a crevice into a dark, dank cave.

A pang of loneliness gripped her, just as it had when she went to a new school at 13 years of age. Every night she had lain in her bed and prayed, "Christ Jesus, I can't bear it any longer. If You love me, why don't You take away this ache in my heart?"

Nothing happened. Soon the salty taste of her prayers turned bitter. She started to suspect, in fact, that God's ears were the four walls and His heart was the empty space in between.

Hurt at His silence, she enacted a swift and childish revenge: She stopped praying, and over the years stopped believing that God cared for her. She sometimes wondered if He even existed.

Five years later she met Tom. Love overwhelmed her with the freshness of spring, blurring the golden sunshine with the blue of his eyes and the thrill of his touch. He was a god to her. She worshiped him, trusting him with heart, mind, and soul.

Three years into their romance, Heather was an unwilling actress in one of those scenes she thought only happened in films. She sat crumpled in the hall of Tom's apartment building. He had said he would be there to meet her, but he wasn't. Except for the sound of his cat crying and clawing at the door, her knocks were answered by silence. His absence confirmed her worst fears, fears that had been building in her for a long time. The lies . . . the deceit . . . the trip with another woman . . . the broken relationship. . . . Deep within her she somehow knew that he was with the other woman. It was over. The hurt of his betrayal sank to the bottom of her heart like lead.

She began to sob. A door opened. Somebody—a man— yelled at her. "If you don't move, I'll call the police!" But where was there to go? Without Tom, her life was empty. Though she was a top college student, and came from a loving and supportive family, at that moment she felt she belonged nowhere. Slowly she struggled back to her feet and walked out into the cold night.

Two weeks later, lying on her back with an oxygen mask over her face, Heather asked herself if it really were too late to trust God. "He would laugh at me if I tried to pray now," she thought. "I turned my back on Him. Why should He take me back now? I don't deserve God's love."

Yet He had saved her life, for on the very evening she had swallowed the pills her mother, feeling disturbed but now knowing of Heather's crisis, had been reading this verse from the Bible: "I call heaven and earth to record this day, that I have set before you life and death, blessing and cursing; therefore choose life, that both you and your seed may live" (Deuteronomy 30:19, KJV).

As her mother read this verse to her in the hospital Heather sensed its significance: God was calling her by name, shining a light into the darkness and reaching down with His strong arms to pull her out. "God wants me to live," she thought.

Could it be that the God she had prayed to as a child, the God who had not answered, cared for her after all? She still felt angry and hurt. She could not reconcile the God of the Bible who loves people with the God of her experience who allows them to suffer. She doubted if she could trust God when she did not understand His ways.

It was the next summer, floating on a lake with her arms dangling over the edge of an air mattress, that Heather's thoughts were suddenly suspended in the expanse of water and sky around her. A small miracle occurred, like a flash of light reflected from a ripple in the water.

Trust filled her being. For the first time she felt able to abandon herself to God, wholeheartedly and completely. Trust came to her as a gift. The sudden realization that broken trust is not restored through intellectual striving or emotional struggle set her free.

From that moment Heather's life was filled with new meaning. The thought that each life is precious to the Lord encouraged her during the months ahead. But sometimes she still battled with feelings of anger and hurt. They stuck to her heart like layers of old wallpaper and would require years of hard work to remove. Healing was not instant. But trusting God, she started to reorganize her life. She began to mature into a beautiful

Christian woman for whom loneliness and rejection were no longer impossibilities, but situations left behind.

Occasionally, though, she still wondered why God had let her go through so much unhappiness. The nagging question of the 13-year-old girl remained: "Christ Jesus, if You love me, why don't You take away the ache in my heart?" But she told herself, "Trust does not demand an answer to this question, but often finds the purpose in the pain."

She didn't understand, but a week before her wedding to a loyal, loving, Christian young man, she caught a glimpse of a possible answer.

She entered the underground station filled with happy thoughts of flowers and vows and hymns. At the far end of the platform she noticed a girl leaning against the wall, occasionally peering into the tunnel in anticipation of the next train. Somehow Heather knew she meant to jump.

"If I'm right," she thought, "I'll save her life. If not, I'll just be embarrassed for a few seconds."

As she approached her, Heather saw that the girl was extremely agitated. Without a moment's hesitation, Heather firmly grasped her shoulders and pulled her away from the edge of the platform. The girl now sobbed uncontrollably.

One train and then another thundered into the station and departed.

Upstairs, over coffee, Heather listened and talked with Vera for several hours. Vera's boyfriend had wanted to end their relationship, and she felt she couldn't live without him.

At last Heather said gently, "No matter what happens, remember that I love you, Vera, and that God loves you. Your life is precious to Him."

And to herself she whispered, "You know that, Heather, beyond a doubt."

The Impossible Achieved

Heather has made a fresh start. Though trust in God and in herself, through the reorganization of her life and her thoughts, and through persistence, life no longer seems impossible. She is one of literally hundreds of people I've known for whom the impossible has been turned into the possible.

I don't know what's impossible to you. Maybe, like Heather, you've had trouble with relationships and can't believe you'll ever find stability and happiness. Or maybe your impossibility lies in a different area—in work, health, age, or womanhood.

Whatever it is, you're probably feeling bad about it.

I was talking to a friend not long ago whose mother, aged 55, is going through a divorce after 28 years of marriage and five children. That good lady is struggling to survive emotionally. Finding meaning and satisfaction for the rest of her life seems to her an insurmountable impossibility.

Facing the impossible can be debilitating. It can lead to depression, produce frustration, and foster unhappiness. And the worse you feel, the more impossible your situation becomes. Dreams recede. Roads to the future are strewn with barbs. The thing that you desperately want to do, to have, or to achieve remains obstinately beyond your reach.

I want you to know there's a way around the impossible.

It begins with the word itself. Be careful what you call impossible—because as soon as you *call* something impossible, you make it so. You become like a person shut in a room who says, "I can't get out, I can't get out!" when all he needs to do is push the door a little harder to find that it gives way.

That "pushing" consists of three things which I call

the TOP principles. TOP stands for: **TRUST, ORGA-NIZE**, and **PERSIST**. The strategy is very straight-forward, and it works. I know because I've road-tested it myself. It has also worked for the many people, famous and not-so-famous, who were kind enough to let me tell their stories in this book.

And it can work for you.

The TOP Test

Do you have the qualities required to turn impossi-bility into opportunity, dead ends into highways? You almost certainly do, even if those strengths are lying dormant and need to be reactivated by putting them to work.

To assess yourself, try the TOP test. Don't take it *too* seriously, since it's meant to loosen you up rather than to provide an exhaustive analysis of your personality. Still, it should function as a spot-check on the strengths you'll need if you're going to face down difficulties from which you would otherwise have shrunk away. And it may tell you where your weaknesses lie.

Simply answer the following questions with a yes or a no. I admit that this is slightly unfair, since to some questions you will probably want to answer "It depends...." Don't worry; just assume there are no other factors bearing on your decision, and do the best you can.

THE TOP TEST

1a. Would you, under any circumstances, be willing to rely on somebody else's opinion in order to make a decision?   Yes/No

1b. Do you keep an appointment book?   Yes/No

1c. In your view, is the proverb "If at first you don't succeed, try, try again" basically sound advice?　Yes/No

2a. Do you seldom doubt your ability to perform a task?　Yes/No

2b. Would you say it is unusual for you to run short of cash because you forgot to go to the bank?　Yes/No

2c. Do you think that Christ's advice to forgive a person "seventy times seven" times should be taken literally?　Yes/No

3a. Would you, without any qualms, give a driver complex directions when you had no map to remind you of the route?　Yes/No

3b. When you go shopping, do you bother to make out a list beforehand?　Yes/No

3c. Is it irksome to you to have to leave a job unfinished?　Yes/No

4a. At work, do you feel a desire to keep a close eye on tasks you have delegated to other people?　Yes/No

4b. If you go to an interview, do you prefer to have some answers worked out in advance?　Yes/No

4c. Does chess appeal to you more than checkers?　Yes/No

5a. Would you lend 100 dollars to a friend, no questions asked?　Yes/No

5b. Can you remember what you had for dinner the night before last?　Yes/No

5c. If you messed up a difficult cake recipe, would you go right back and do it again rather than choosing something easier?   Yes/No

6a. Would you say you feel safe in the care of doctors?   Yes/No

6b. Does Monopoly appeal to you more than Trivial Pursuit?   Yes/No

6c. Would you argue with somebody who told you the U.S. should have abandoned the shuttle program after the Challenger disaster?   Yes/No

7a. Do you see your life going well rather than badly over the next ten years?   Yes/No

7b. If a family member said, "You're always losing things!" would you feel this to be unjust?   Yes/No

7c. Would you willingly put in extra hours at a task you didn't like, for the sake of getting the job done?   Yes/No

8a. Are you often satisfied with your own performance?   Yes/No

8b. Would you feel irritated working in an untidy office?   Yes/No

8c. Do you think that, in general, it is worth making a sacrifice for something you want?   Yes/No

9a. In your opinion, are you trustworthy?   Yes/No

9b. Do you seek to adjust your way of working in order to achieve greater efficiency?   Yes/No

9c. Do you tend to finish a book once
you've started reading it?   Yes/No

10a. In difficult situations do you get
comfort from the thought that
"somehow I will be given the strength
to get through"?   Yes/No

10b. Would you enjoy organizing party
games for children?   Yes/No

10c. Do you deny that you're easily bored?   Yes/No

To evaluate your answers, first add up separately the number of "yes" answers you gave for "a" questions, "b" questions, and "c" questions. The scores run on a scale of 0 to 10, with 5 indicating the average. The higher the scores are, the more you tend toward trust, organization, and persistence.

How do you shape up?

Whatever the result, bear in mind that the TOP test tells you where you are *now*, and not where you might be six months from now. That is very important, because even if you register zero on all three scales that is no worse than having an X-ray reveal a broken wrist: It gives you the information you need to choose the right next step.

Your TOP test may uncover a weak area you've suspected or known about for a long time. You may discover you are better, for example, at organizing than persisting.

But why trust, organize, and persist at all? What makes those three qualities so special in tackling the impossible?

Trust

The Bible contains a passage that is profoundly relevant to the issue of trust.

Do you remember how the Israelites in the Old Testament, when they came close to the Promised Land, decided to send spies ahead of them? The spies came back with a mixture of good news and bad. The land, they had discovered, was a virtual paradise. "It flows with milk and honey," they said, "and this is its fruit." They showed their countrymen samples of fruit they had brought back with them.

Then they broke the bad news: "But the people who live in the land are very strong. The cities are huge, with strong walls. And what's more, we saw the descendants of Anak there...."

Now you should know that in their time the descendants of Anak were a bit like Rambo—not the kind of people you want to pick a fight with. Therefore the overall picture which the spies brought back was bleak. Sure, the land was rich and productive, but it was so well-defended that for the Israelites to think of attacking it was sheer folly. After all, they had brought virtually nothing with them from Egypt in the way of arms, since they were a nomadic people. They traveled light, and they had their wives and children and cattle with them. How on earth were they supposed to go in and do battle with well-armed giants? It was an impossible undertaking.

We understand their plight because we too have been in similar straits ourselves and reacted in much the same way.

But notice something important about this story: *Nobody listening to the spies' report had been to the Promised Land.* Therefore, nobody except the spies could form an opinion on the basis of firsthand observation. When the people discussed the descendants of Anak, they were speaking the language of myth, not fact. Even the spies were conveying only a visual impression: "We were like grasshoppers in our own sight, and so we were in their sight" (Numbers 13:33).

Similarly, not many of us can comprehend with complete, cool objectivity the real proportions of the impossible. We are forced, whether we like it or not, to trust someone else's view. But this immediately confronts us with a question: Whom are we going to trust? The pessimists? Or the optimists—the Calebs who say at the borders of Canaan, "Let us go up at once and take possession, for we are well able to overcome it" (Numbers 13:30)?

But Trust Whom?

As Christians we have the guidance of the Holy Spirit, who promises to lead us into all truth. With reliance on Him we trust our own judgment—not that of others with their questionable agenda.

If you have a problem with what I've said about trusting yourself, let me remind you that you do it every day. You trust yourself in your talking, driving, and even in making the coffee. Do you ever doubt your competence to put coffee granules in a cup? Don't get me wrong— I'm not equating cooking breakfast and running a multinational conglomerate. My point is that if you trust yourself implicitly in simple things, you are capable of trusting yourself in all things.

But self-trust is only a foundation. Few great feats are accomplished by one man or one woman standing alone. We all need help. Realizing our dependence on other people is one of the keys to doing the impossible. Take, for example, the human rights activist Martin Luther King, Jr.

Many people think of King as a voice crying in the wilderness, a single man struggling against the attitudes of a nation. And it is true that as a black man he was in the minority. His people did not hold the reins of power and had every reason to distrust those who did. Yet, as a leader devoted to peaceful protest, Martin Luther

King, Jr. displayed an enormous amount of trust not only in blacks but in the whole racial mix of the U.S.A. You may recall part of a speech he gave in 1963:

> I say to you today, my friends, that in spite of the difficulties and frustrations of the moment I still have a dream . . . I have a dream that one day in the red hills of Georgia the sons of former slaves and the sons of former slave owners will be able to sit down together at the table of brotherhood . . . of that day when all God's children, black men and white men, Jews and Gentiles, Protestants and Catholics, will be able to join hands and sing in the words of the old Negro spiritual, "Free at last! Free at last! Thank God Almighty, we are free at last!"

Martin Luther King, Jr., wasn't the first person to engage in a momentous task and "thank God Almighty" for the power to see it through. After the United States won its independence, Benjamin Franklin told the Constitutional Convention of 1787:

> I believe that Providence guides the affairs of men, and never a sparrow falls to the ground that God does not attend its funeral, and that all the hairs of our heads are numbered. I don't believe that an empire or a republic can be launched without His help, and I move, Mr. President, that this Convention open with prayer, and that we petition Divine guidance and help in the step we are about to take.

"All things," said Jesus, "are possible to him who believes" (Mark 9:23). Notice, He said "All things." Jesus was talking about an impossible problem: The child whose condition He referred to was epileptic. There was no treatment for epilepsy in those days, and the seizures had often threatened to kill the boy by throwing him into deep water or a fire. Yet to the helpless father Jesus said, "*All things* are possible." The boy was healed.

The original Greek word for "possible" as used by Jesus was *dunatos*. "Possible" is in fact a weak translation; the word held a robust, almost physical connotation, of power rather than mere opportunity. "All options are within the grasp" might better communicate the meaning.

One interpretation of this concept is that for the person who believes (and even for those, like the father of the epileptic, who confess their unbelief) prayer will be answered by divine intervention. Sometimes that's true, but not always: More often the hand of God, though active, stays hidden in the currents of natural cause-and-effect. In this way the story of the Blue Bird Company is typical of trust in God.

The Luce brothers (George, Albert, and Joe), owners of Blue Bird of Fort Valley, Georgia, first realized their need of a thousand-ton press in 1957.

I assume the press was necessary to keep the business viable and its market share adequate. Even more than that, it was necessary to maintain the momentum of a business launched in prayer and dedicated to God. Read *Wings of Bluebird*, the story of the company, and you're forced to the conclusion that the parents, Lawrence and Helen Luce, looked upon the company as more than a business to provide their livelihood; they looked upon it as an employer of people in Fort Valley who needed work. In addition, they saw in it the opportunity to strengthen and expand God's work around the world.

Lawrence possessed a gift of vision and Helen had the gift of encouragement. Both were people of prayer. What a duo! The story of the Blue Bird Bus Company is a litany of impossibilities that were turned into possibilities through trust, organization, and persistence. In

1927, they made one bus. Ten years later, they manufactured more school buses than any company in the world.

The sons have carried on in the great tradition of their remarkable parents.

Against this backdrop you can see that the need for the press was more than a frivolous desire.

Still, they had set themselves a tough assignment. George Luce explained to me that the thousand-ton press has a five-by-ten-foot bed and a 30-inch stroke. By any reckoning that's a big piece of machinery. At that time the Luce brothers couldn't afford to buy a new press, and even though they made several trips to Detroit to evaluate used equipment, by the time they convened a planning meeting on January 1, 1958, they had heard of only one secondhand machine that met their specifications. The problem was that it was owned by the Ford Motor Company.

Since Ford seemed unlikely to part with a four-year-old press, Buddy Luce concluded, "Somewhere God has the right press for us. Let's keep praying that it'll come available."

Days later they got a call from an old associate of their father's, a machinery dealer in Baltimore. Somehow he had heard about their search, and he had some good news. "That press will come on the market in a few weeks. I know a couple of freelance dealers in Detroit. Trust them, and do what they tell you, and you will get it."

It all worked out exactly as he said. The Luce brothers obtained the press—which matched their specifications in every significant area—for about one-third of the manufacturer's price. In due time it was installed at the Blue Bird plant in Fort Valley, where to this day it is producing parts for buses.

Organize

Read to the end of the story in the Gospel of Mark

9:14-29, and you'll find an intriguing exchange between Jesus and His disciples. The disciples, perhaps a little piqued at their failure to help the epileptic lad, asked Jesus why they couldn't drive out the spirit of epilepsy.

Jesus' reply? "This kind can come out by nothing but prayer and fasting."

Here we pass beyond trust. Jesus, the God-man, trusted God the Father, as presumably the disciples also did. But in this instance simple trust was insufficient to effect a healing. Trust had to be supplemented by a *disciplined spirituality*.

A close look at the Gospels reveals that Jesus systematically undergirded His public ministry with retreat and private prayer. It's a good pattern to follow. Just as important, it serves as an example of the general truth that *you must organize if you are to achieve*. I suspect that this is the common denominator of all achievers. Strip away the biographical detail, and you'll find that every one of them has at some point set a goal and then devised a strategy to achieve it.

Why set goals? Simply because goal-setting is the antithesis of immobility. Anyone who's had an impossible problem will know how tempting it is to just sit there and stare at it. As long as you are staring at the problem with its long shadow of dismal consequences, you are no nearer a solution. Although unhappiness and discontent are powerful motivators, they cannot give direction. Goals can.

Sally and John, for instance, faced the all-too-common "impossibility" of getting their teenagers safely through adolescence. They have four girls, so they knew it could be tough! Long before the issue of late-night parties came around, however, Sally and John decided that one of their goals was to give the girls a firm sense of responsibility. At age 15 the eldest daughter, Tammie, asked to stay out late Saturday night. Everyone knew it was a drinking party. But Sally and John realized that by answering the question "yes" or "no" they would be giving Tammie an excuse—either to go as a sign of rebellion or to stay away and blame her absence on her parents.

"Do you think it's a good idea to go to that kind of party?" they asked her.

"Why not?"

"Would you be happy for us to go to the kind of party put on by our neighbors down the street—like the one raided by the police a couple months ago?"

"Oh, but that was a drug scene. There won't be any drugs here. Honest."

"Tammie, ask yourself the question, 'Does Bill Jones, the senior class president you think is so neat, go to that kind of party?"

Tammie didn't go.

Is Your Goal SMART?

Certain principles exist that distinguish a good goal-setting program from a poor one. There are many programs available. My favorite has been devised by Paul J. Meyer, founder of the renowned Success Motivation Institute in Waco, Texas.[1] According to Paul Meyer, goals should be: Specific, Measurable, Attainable, Realistic, Tangible.

```
┌─────────────────────────────┐
│   GOAL-SETTING IN THE       │
│   S-M-A-R-T MODE            │
└─────────────────────────────┘
```

1. SPECIFIC.

Goals should be specific steps, not vague desires. An unfocused goal is useless. Saying "I want to honor the Lord" is an unfocused goal even though it may stimulate the praise of your friends. Resolving to found a voluntary agency geared to help people with HIV infection may get you no praise at all, but it'll surely move you off the starting blocks.

2. MEASURABLE.

"If you can't measure it, you can't monitor it," says Meyer. You should make your goals measurable not just in terms of *what* is accomplished but also *when*. It was on this principle that Haggai Institute committed to train 10,000 Third World leaders by the year A.D. 2000. That long-term goal is broken down into short-term intermediary goals. That's how I know we're on target.

3. ATTAINABLE.

I could have set out to train every church member in the world, or build a chain of luxury hotels in Siberia, or teach my dog to sing arias from Handel's *Messiah*. But I didn't do so because I know that these goals are beyond my (and certainly my dog's) ability. That's not to discourage ambition.

4. REALISTIC.

Be realistic in your timing; don't go for too much too soon. Losing 20 pounds may be attainable, but to do so in 24 hours is not realistic. Putting a man on the moon was attainable. Doing it within 12 months after President Kennedy announced the goal was not realistic. The NASA space program didn't begin with a frenzied rush. The man-on-the-moon objective was worked toward gradually, each of the thousands of steps becoming intermediate goals and each goal building on the previous one, until in 1969 Neil Alden Armstrong stepped off the landing module to make his "giant leap for mankind."

5. TANGIBLE.

A tangible goal is one that demands an immediate change in behavior or planning. A man whose marriage is going through some rough times could back up the long-term goal of treating his wife more considerately by making some short-term resolutions: "For the next seven days I won't complain when she's late" or "For the next month I'll take her out to dinner every Friday night."

Persist

The SMART program gives a lot more good advice on goal-setting than I have room to pass on here (see chapter 2 of my book *Lead On!* for a fuller treatment on goal-setting).

One feature that should be obvious from the summary above is the stress it lays on continuity. The eyes of a goal-setter are firmly fixed on the horizon—on the result he or she wants to achieve at the end of the program. At the same time, though, it recognizes that human beings have a short attention span. Contemplation of remote goals reverts all too easily to a glum staring at the impossible problem.

The SMART solution to this tendency is simply to break up a long journey into short trips, the arduous ascent into single steps. No section of the program is overwhelmingly hard, and each completed section brings you one step nearer your final destination.

But even when using this "staircase" technique you'll need the third TOP quality—that of *persistence*. Christopher Columbus, for example, quickly discovered that even his intermediate goals required some hard negotiating. After all, he wasn't going to make a pioneering journey around the globe without financial backing.

In the course of nearly a decade he negotiated, lengthily but unsuccessfully, with both the King of Portugal and the Count of Medina. He finally won the support of Ferdinand and Isabella, rulers of Castille in Spain. That Columbus was still holding out for high terms by this stage is remarkable (he wanted to be made admiral immediately, and viceroy of all the lands he discovered); that the terms were accepted is nearly miraculous. But accepted they were, and so it was that Columbus set sail on April 3, 1492, on his next intermediate goal—the difficult one of reaching America.

Persistence is essential to success. I will never forget the story that Bob Pierce, founder of World Vision, told me about a clergyman he had met as a young man. The clergyman said to Pierce, "I have studied leaders and organizations. I have devoured biographies and autobiographies. I have immersed myself in history. I have carefully observed the contemporary leadership of my day. And I have come to the conclusion that one factor distinguishes the organization that wins: *staying power*."

A business friend of mine who realized the importance of having a telephone number that is easily remembered contacted the telephone operator in his city to ask if he could have the number 343-0123.

"Sir," the operator replied, "I really don't think that's possible, because those numbers are already taken."

"Have you tried?" he asked.

She hadn't. When she did, lo and behold, the number was available. He then asked for a matching number on his home phone: 344-0123.

She laughed and said, "Sir, you know that's not possible because all of those numbers are taken. You couldn't possibly get two in a row like that."

"Just try."

She came back embarrassed. "I cannot believe this, but the second number is available too!"

"Thank you kindly," said my friend. "You've been a great help to me today."

How easy it would have been for him to share the operator's pessimism! That's exactly what most folks do; when the impossible confronts them, they give up before they even try. They don't give themselves the chance to succeed because they've decided in advance that they can't.

There's an old ad man's motto: *The difficult we do immediately; the impossible takes a little longer*. It is that "little longer" that you cover with the strength of persistence.

The TOP Principles

Trust. Organize. Persist.
- Cultivate an appropriate trust in God, in yourself, and in those around you.
- Organize a well-structured goals program.
- Don't give up.

Those are the three secrets of overcoming the impossible—the TOP principles.

How are you going to implement them? I'll be honest with you—there's no magic involved. The TOP principles won't jump off the page and reorder your life just because you've read enough to know what they are.

Basic to any kind of endeavor is *commitment*. If you don't have that, there's nothing I or anybody else can do to help you.

What does commitment mean? One of the best explanations I've found is in a letter written by the founder of the Little Brothers of Jesus, Charles de Foucauld. Foucauld had embarked on the dangerous adventure of exploring Morocco, disguised as a Moroccan Jew, at a time when the country was closed to Europeans. He wrote these words to his sister: "When you start out to accomplish something, you must not come back until you have done it." Sound advice.

The rest of this book aims to do two things. One is to look in more detail at the different kinds of impossibility. The other is to show how the TOP principles can make "impossible" an obsolete word.

2

SUCCESSFUL STUDY

Gloria and her husband, Bill, had graduated from one of America's most prestigious Christian colleges. Friends considered them the ideal Christian couple. He was on the staff of a prominent Christian organization working with youth. Later he went into business.

By the age of 40 they lived in a palatial home in one of America's high-income suburbs where they reared four lovely children. They had all the trappings of wealth: lakeside home, boat, expensive cars, designer clothes—the works.

Suddenly, as if out of nowhere, divorce torpedoed the seeming solidarity of their home.

Gloria moved South. To support her four children she took a teaching job. The salary was so meager that she qualified for welfare. While she got minimum alimony, the financial demands on her were unbearable. For instance, during the years of their marriage, her ex-husband bought properties and required her to cosign the mortgages. After the divorce he had not paid taxes, so the mortgagers came after her to pay. A number of times they tried to get her into court to pay bills she hadn't incurred.

A clinical psychologist visited her class and became intrigued by some of her unusual work with discipline. He asked her to work with him in the counseling center doing psychological testing on children. He then said, "You don't need to be a teacher; you need to prepare for a career in psychology. I'll give you a start."

She worked full-time and pursued her master's degree with evening studies.

Just as she was getting into the swing of her new regimen she was a victim in an auto accident. A truck hit her car from the back and damaged two of her lower vertebrae. She was off her feet for seven months, but through sheer determination finished her master's degree while still in bed.

Then a doctor, a friend of the family who had known Gloria since she was a little girl, offered her a little office to start her counseling practice. She started with one person as a client, and then that person told another. Her practice gradually increased until today it's flourishing.

By the time this book is in your hands she will have earned her Ph.D. in the field of psychology.

Today her two older children are married, and she still has two at home. Now in her fifties, she faces the prospect of a fulfilling vocation with sufficient income to meet the needs of the family.

She turned an impossibility into a possibility.

How and Why

Gloria is just one of many people who have proved that the TOP principles work in the real-life area of studies. She told me she trusted God for wisdom to make the right decisions. She relied heavily on the promise of James 1:5: "If any of you lacks wisdom, let him ask of God, who gives to all liberally and without reproach, and it will be given him." She organized her time and resources. She showed uncomplaining persistence.

You may be facing similar impossibilities. Formal study can bring financial hardship. You may have to work part-time and sacrifice precious hours of leisure. You may have heavy burdens of responsibility already— for instance, a couple of children—or be under strong pressure from your peers or your spouse not to "waste time on something you probably can't do anyway."

Study, of course, doesn't have to mean taking a college course and ending up with a degree. You may want to teach yourself techniques of watercolor painting, read more widely, or go into greater depth with your study of the Bible. These aren't necessarily any less intimidating. Perhaps you're afraid of study in any form, especially if you regard yourself as "not the intellectual type," or are advanced in age, or out of practice. To you, completing a course of study will seem like swimming the length of the Mississippi River against the current.

Don't lose heart—you can turn impossibilities into possibilities.

First of all, identify a specific goal. That may be easy if you're taking a college course, since the long-term goal is the final qualification and the medium-term goals are the completion of the modules. With personal study, goals are more fluid and therefore more important to pin down. You will need to consider how much time you have available every week and where you can place markers to measure your progress. You might choose to read and take notes from 12 books on clothes design in one year, or to reach a certain grade level in piano proficiency in six months, or to complete eight two-hour sessions each night in learning to use a word processor.

It is particularly helpful at this stage to be clear about your motivation.

Most people approach education with the question *How?* when first of all they should be asking *Why?* What lies at the end of the reading schedule, the doctoral dissertation, or the evening class in Japanese flower-arranging? Why are you bothering to do it in the first place?

I'm not nitpicking here; too many people get involved in study because their friends are doing it or because of some vague notion in their heads that studying is "good" for them. I don't dispute the idea that education is good, since Proverbs says, "How much better it is to get wisdom than gold! And to get understanding is to be chosen rather than silver" (Proverbs 16:16). Nor am I such a purist as to insist that your motives be exclusively academic. Life is too short for that.

Be clear on your reasons.

- Are you seeking a skill as a basis for your future career?

- Are you looking for a professional qualification that will further the career you have already embarked on?

- Are you simply interested in the subject for its own sake?

- Do you need an intellectual challenge?

- Do you want to have the experience of being a student and the special opportunities that status brings?

- Are you less interested in studying than in making new friends?

- Do you feel that in comparison to taking an unrewarding job, study is the lesser of two evils?

- Are you doing it to fulfill someone else's expectations of you?

Any of these reasons can be valid. What matters is to *recognize your reasons and be happy with them.* If part of your motive in going to business school is to please a friend, that's fine as long as you agree with the idea and make a goal of it. Pleasing a friend would not be a valid reason if you went off to business school seething with resentment that your main objective is to study Portuguese literature.

Drivers and Passengers

There are two ways to approach study. You can drive, or you can sit in the passenger seat and watch the scenery go by.

Winston Churchill, by his own account, spent most of his early youth in the passenger seat:

> I wrote my name at the top of the page. I wrote down the number of the question "1." After much reflection, I put a bracket around it thus: "(1)." But thereafter I could not think of anything connected with it that was either relevant or true.... It was from these slender indications of scholarship that Mr. Welldon drew the conclusion that I was worthy to pass into Harrow. It is very much to his credit.[1]

By the same age, Horace Mann almost certainly knew less than Churchill. But both men became drivers. Though before the age of 15 Mann had never attended school more than ten weeks in a year, at age 20 it took him only six months to gain admission to the sophomore class at Brown University, where three years later he graduated with highest honors.

Mann practiced law and then returned to the university to teach Latin and Greek and to serve as librarian before taking an interest in public affairs. In the Massachusetts legislature he became Secretary of the Board of Education. His educational program for the state made the Massachusetts system a prototype for the whole United States. Mann became a U.S. Congressman at 52, and finally President of Antioch College in Yellow Springs, Ohio. His last words to students, delivered in a baccalaureate address only weeks before his death, were: "Be ashamed to die until you have won some victory for humanity."

A 19-Year-Old Driver

He was barely 19 years old, a fugitive from North Korea, trying desperately to stay ahead of the invading Communists. The year was 1950, and he had fled all the way to the southern part of Korea.

But the Communists caught him and bound him. He was desperate, and with a herculean effort he managed to break free. He was fleeing through the forest when a Communist gun barked. Just as the executioner pulled the trigger, the young man, Won Sul Lee, stumbled so that the bullet only grazed the back of his head.

Friends invited him to hide out in their humble home. During that episode Won Sul Lee promised the Lord to follow Him faithfully the rest of his life.

To do the will of God, as he was led to understand it, required him to get an education. But who would finance him? His father, a Christian minister, had no funds. Won Sul Lee couldn't study in his native North Korea, since authorities there sought his life. And war had shut down the schools in the southern part of Korea.

Against the most incredible odds, he proceeded. He never was a passenger—only a driver.

In 1955 Dr. Douglas Cozart, now my colleague (Vice-President of Third World Relations for Haggai Institute), gave Won Sul Lee 150 dollars so he could leave for America and pursue his education. At the time Doug made the gift, Won Sul Lee had only five dollars in cash in his pocket. Yet less than six years later he had three degrees: B.A., M.A., and Ph.D.

He received his B.A. in political science from Ohio Northern University, and his M.A. and his Ph.D. in history from Case Western.

During all that time he had to support his family by working at any job available. Once he took a job cleaning out latrines to earn a few dollars. Later he worked in the library.

Before the Korean war had broken out, prior to his coming to America for graduate training, he had done undergraduate work at Yonsei University. He had also studied at the Korean Presbyterian Seminary.

He never felt the call of God to be a preacher of the gospel, but he wanted to have a thorough grounding in the Scriptures. He told me, "Because of my suffering during the war, I wanted to know more of the Lord, so I went to seminary."

Before he was 35 years of age, in 1965, he was appointed Director of the Higher Education Bureau in the ministry of education in Korea. He had jurisdiction over all of South Korea's universities and colleges. Kyung Hee University, a school with over 20,000 students, elected him Dean of its Graduate School in 1975 and Vice-President in 1980.

He turned down the proffered presidency of that school a few years later.

Also he was made the Secretary General of the International Association of University Presidents.

Today he serves as President of the Han Nam University in Taejon, Korea. However, he lectures on all continents. In the late 70's he served as Chairman of Faculties for Haggai Institute, an organization to which he still lends his expertise and dedication.

He has been a trailblazer in the area of education, both secular and religious. For example, he has instituted in his university a series of studies that acquaint the students with the Bible. There are such courses as "The Bible and Economics," "The Bible and Literature," and "The Bible and History."

Only 23 percent of the students are Christians when they enter Han Nam University. More than 50 percent confess Christ when they graduate.

Dr. Won Sul Lee has written 14 books, half of them in English. He edited a newspaper column for nine years. He has produced scores of monographs.

He set his course and achieved his goal.

You Get What You Insist On

During the 1940's a young woman in India by the name of Grace Sathyaraj had the unusual ambition of following an academic career. But a university ordinance stood in her way: She had failed part of her crucial intermediate examinations and couldn't take the exam again without spending another year at school. She knew this was impossible for her, so she protested. But she was unsuccessful.

In the course of the following year she married. Family opposition to her plan, always strong, now became implacable.

In fact, because it was thought improper for a wife to be more qualified than her husband, she was forced by her father-in-law to take up secondary-school-teacher training. Nevertheless, Grace Sathyaraj, like Winston Churchill, was a driver. She persisted in her attempt to gain entrance to the university, and in the end pestered the university office so much that they advised her to appeal to the Vice-Chancellor. Only her father would stand by her, and together they went to see him.

The Vice-Chancellor, who wasn't easily moved by appeals of this kind, asked her why she wanted to study. "What difference will this make now that you are married?"

Grace answered, "I will never stop studying; therefore I want to appear for the examination." Grace was determined to prepare herself to be the best school principal possible. Furthermore, she said it was her passion to bring the ultimate credibility to her Christian witness, and she felt education would help achieve that goal.

He let her take the exam. She passed, and she is studying to this day. Now a grandmother, she will have received her doctorate in 1989.

In the next few sections of this chapter let's look at some techniques that will help you organize your study. For a start, we might ask what study is.

The Techniques of Learning

From the outside, learning looks like one single process. In fact it is not. When we learn, we use a combination of techniques which, because they don't belong to any particular subject, can be applied to *all* subjects.

Benjamin Bloom in his book *Taxonomy of Educational Objectives* identifies five techniques of learning.[2] These can be summarized as follows:

COMPREHENSION. Take as an example the statement "All human beings are either introverts or extroverts." You almost certainly know what is meant by the terms "introvert" and "extrovert" and understand that the statement is generalizing from them. In other words, the assertion means something to you. You comprehend it.

APPLICATION. It is possible to comprehend statements (or ideas, or arguments, or books) that are untrue. "All cats are green" is a false statement, but that doesn't stop you from comprehending it. How do you know it's false? By *application*. The statement doesn't match up to experience: Cats come in a good many colors but never in green.

EVALUATION. To evaluate something is to judge its value for a given purpose. Ogden Nash's poem on fleas

Adam
had 'em

may or may not be a strict literal truth. In terms of humor and succinctness, however, it rates highly. Try applying the statement about introverts and extroverts to your own circle of friends. Is it true, partially true, or a gross generalization? If it's true, would it be a good way to choose candidates for drama school?

ANALYSIS. All of the statements above are short and easily comprehended. Longer works, like Shakespeare's *Macbeth*, need to be "broken down." Structure, concepts, themes, patterns, language, character, and style (to name but a few) each become separate subjects of comprehension and evaluation.

SYNTHESIS. "Can all human beings be categorized as introverts or extroverts?" is a question demanding synthesis. To answer it, for example as an essay, you might bring together ideas about the precise meaning of the terms used, previous studies in which the statement has been applied, alternative models of human personality, and so on. Molding these into a single argument (in this case an evaluation) is a process of synthesis.

Paper Space

"Of making many books there is no end," concludes the writer of Ecclesiastes glumly, "and much study is a weariness of the flesh" (Ecclesiastes 12:12).

He is right on both counts. Like it or not, knowledge is passed on through books. Since you cannot possibly read all of the books available on any given subject, you must be selective in your reading. This changes the impossibility of reading everything on a given subject into the possibility of reading what is most important on the subject. Also, you need to read in the most efficient manner possible.

Note: *most efficient*, not quickest. The object is not to reach the back cover before lunch, but to find in the book exactly the information you're looking for. Before you pick it up, therefore, you need a clear idea of what you want to know. Of course there are a few excellent books which you'll want to wade through not just once but several times. However, this is rare. Most books are like shops: You go in and find the item you want—you don't buy up the whole store.

A number of reading techniques have been developed, among them Robinson's SQ3R (Survey, Question, Read, Recall, Review). I like this technique adapted from Buzan.

EFFICIENT READING[3]

- OVERVIEW. Use the book's own "entry" system—the contents page. Browse over chapter headings, illustrations, photos, and tables. Skim it to get a long-range impression.

- PREVIEW. Zoom in on the chapters relevant to you. Concentrate particularly on opening paragraphs (of chapters or sections), since most writers tend to summarize ideas here.

- INVIEW. Move on from relevant opening paragraphs to follow the ideas further. Aim to comprehend the argument of a complete section or chapter without getting bogged down in complexities. Get a feel for the place of this section in the wider sweep of the book.

- REVIEW. Now move back to work through the difficult passages (you should know by now whether this is worth the time). Make notes summarizing the writer's ideas. Make quotations short, apt, and memorable, not forgetting to note the page number. At the end—or in the margin as you go—jot down your evaluation of what you've read.

Ear Space

For many students, taking notes from lectures can be the hardest part of the course. The difficulty may lie in the subtlety of the topic (a lecture on calculus, for instance, would lose me in the first 30 seconds). On the other hand, the difficulty may lie in the presentation. Most lectures do not start, like a sermon, by promising to cover the ground in three points. Those that do make life a lot easier. Those that don't can still be understood. Points in a lecture operate much like paragraphs in a book, and when a lecturer goes from one point to the next, he or she generally takes a quick breather and then supplies a linking sentence. To take a random example, in a lecture about the budget deficit, the words "...one key effect of American fiscal policy has been on the pattern of international trade..." clearly indicate a change of direction.

Occam's Razor and Occam's Shave

Occam's razor is a principle originated by the medieval philosopher William of Occam. He put it like this:

ENTIA NON SUNT MULTIPLICANDA PRATER NECESSITATEM

It means—and I'm not translating literally—that of two equally effective solutions to a problem the *simpler* one is better.

Look at Figure 2.1, Occam's Razor in Action. It's upside down. Why? At least two explanations will have occurred to you. One is that the production editor, the proofreader, and the printer of this book all have such appalling eyesight that they didn't notice the problem. The other possible explanation is that the illustration was placed upside down *deliberately* at the author's request. Both scenarios adequately explain the result, but you will agree that the second is more likely than the first, because it requires fewer speculative assumptions: Statistically the odds are longer on three people missing an inconsistency than on one person wanting to introduce it.

Occam's razor is one of several techniques useful in problem-solving. Another is Guilford's distinction between *divergent thinking* and *convergent thinking*. Let

ENTIA NON SUNT MULTIPLICANDA
PRATER NECESSITATEM

Figure 2.1: Occam's Razor in Action

me illustrate the way these work by quoting from the last chapter of an imaginary whodunit:

> Inspector Clam allowed himself the luxury of a slight pause before he reached the climax of his story. He lit a cigarette, flipping the chrome lighter back into the pocket of his crumpled trench coat as he took the first drag.
>
> "But that left the problem of a motive," he said. He frowned. "Why would Colonel Linchgrit want to shoot a hotel cook? Jealousy? Blackmail? Anger at finding a fly in his soup? None of these seemed likely. And then, quite by accident, I came on this letter..." He held up the torn envelope. "It is addressed to your sister, Colonel—but you forgot to post it. It says, and I quote: 'Finally I have found that traitor Merrick, working (would you believe it?) as third chef here at the Palace Hotel. I have waited a long time for this. You know what they say—*too many cooks spoil the broth....*'"
>
> Calmly refolding the letter, Inspector Clam cast a grim glance around the room. "From that I could draw only one conclusion. That you, Colonel, were the bearded nun seen entering the kitchen with a shotgun last Thursday night."

Pursuing a motive for the murder, Inspector Clam uses *divergent thinking*. Given the facts implicating Colonel Linchgrit, his mind generates a series of reasons why this apparently upright citizen should creep into the kitchen disguised as a nun and shoot the third chef. He is, as Guilford puts it, "looking for logical possibilities." The vital clue comes in the letter, and the Colonel's hints of a previous and ill-fated relationship with Merrick. Given this knowledge, Inspector Clam then uses *convergent thinking*. If circumstantial evidence points to the

Colonel, and the Colonel has a proven motive, then the one and only conclusion must be that the Colonel committed the crime.

Unless you happen to be a storybook detective, the chances are that you will feel more at home with one kind of thinking than the other. But you actually need both, because different occasions demand different forms of mental agility. Sometimes you will need to "brainstorm" to get ideas; other times you will have to work out what follows, as a matter of necessity, from information you already possess.

I Don't Have the Money!

For many people the impossibility of study is not academic but financial: They just can't afford it.

I can identify with that, because from start to finish my father couldn't give me a cent toward my college education. Experience has taught me that without independent means, student life can be tough. But it's rarely impossible. The key to financial survival is good organization.

Make this your first exercise in problem-solving. Get out a pen and a sheet of blank paper, and work it out. How much more money per year would you have to pay out if you were studying? Divide that amount by 52 to get the weekly figure and enter that figure at the top of column X below. Underneath, fill in your present estimated weekly expenditure on each item:

	X	Y
1. The course of study:		
2. Food:		
3. Housing:		
4. Utilities		
5. Clothing:		
6. Debt repayment:		
7. Transportation:		

8. Social: _____ _____
9. ? _____ _____
10. ? _____ _____
11. ? _____ _____
12. ? _____ _____

TOTAL: _____ _____

Now ask yourself this: "How badly do I want an education?"

If you would be happy doing something else, that's fine. But if you really want an education—want it badly enough that you're prepared to make sacrifices—go back to the table and fill in column Y. This time don't put down the present figures, but a Spartan budget—the lowest estimate possible without endangering yourself or your family. A lot of people live on less than that for most of their lives. Can you manage it for three or four years?

Next, do a little brainstorming. You want to find a weekly income that exceeds the total for column Y. Search out every alternative: working during vacation, working in the evenings, maximizing income, saving and investing for a couple of years and using the investment to get you through the course. Consider squeezing extra hours from your social schedule in order to work or study. Perhaps you're eligible for a grant or scholarship. Do everything you can think of to bump up that weekly income to the level you need.

Above all, pray! Trust God for wisdom to know what to do and for the grace to do it.

International Student

Sam (not his real name) was 21 years old and headed for national service in the Mideastern nation of his birth.

The average Westerner doesn't know that certain religious fanatics in national power deliberately place Christians in the most dangerous positions. That was the situation in Sam's country. So he fled to Beirut.

Since he hadn't notified the authorities of his departure, he was considered a refugee from their style of justice.

It had been a tough struggle ever since his last year of secondary school (high school in American terminology). A severe case of typhoid illness in his senior year robbed Sam of several months of schooling, so he had to repeat his last year.

In that nation, as in most commonwealth countries, students at primary and secondary schools wear a required uniform. It was humiliating for this well-built, mature young man to trudge in his uniform with the little children to the secondary school while his peer group in casual clothes would meet him on their way to the university. But he swallowed his pride, determined not only that he would finish his secondary education with honors, but also that he would get the best education attainable anywhere in the world.

In Beirut he met the only person he knew, a Syrian evangelist whom he had met in his hometown. During his brief Beirut tenure the evangelist encouraged him and prayed with him.

The young fugitive knew that every day he tarried in that part of the world increased his danger.

He borrowed 600 dollars to move to Australia. Upon arrival, he had only 100 dollars left. Despite his extremely halting English, he managed to get a job as a technical assistant with the telephone company, Australian Telecom.

Within 18 months he and Margaret (not her real name), an Australian schoolteacher, fell in love and married. With her hard-earned salary and his painstaking study, he graduated from Moore College. That in itself seemed an impossibility at first. In fact, at the beginning of his second year the academic dean insisted on the school's discharging the young foreigner because of his defective English. But the determined Arab never gave up. Today the school heralds him as an illustrious alumnus. The academic dean, a close friend, now seeks the former student's counsel.

After graduation, Sam served for 2¹/₂ years as curate in a prestigious Anglican parish in a Sydney suburb. He then sold all his possessions and moved with wife and baby to California to work on a master's degree at Fuller Seminary.

Maintaining his studies and supporting his growing family ate up his entire savings and forced him to sell his little secondhand car.

His next move was to Atlanta to assume an executive post with an international organization and earn his Ph.D. at Emory University.

Today he is recognized as an international scholar and leader. Leaders of nations on six continents and heads of media news departments (print and electronic) seek his advice on geopolitical matters. Theologians and missiologists many years his senior sit at his feet.

Within eight years after he fled from his native land, the famed Mideastern president invited him back for a personal visit.

Talk about impossibilities! For more than a decade the young fugitive lived in the cocoon of the impossible. But he refused to listen to his fears. Though Sam is given neither to sanctimonious drivel nor to supersaint trigger words, after minutes in this young Arab's company, the most casual observer recognizes his unshakable confidence in God.

In each episode of his odyssey he planned and organized as thoroughly as possible.

He never gave up.

By the grace of God he turned an impossibility into a possibility.

As a result of his TOP performance, millions of people around the world are influenced for God and for good by his sermons, lectures, and writings (both fiction and nonficton).

Because his life is under constant threat, I can't reveal his real name, but that's not important. His life and work are all-important.

The TOP Student

TRUST. If you feel overwhelmed at the prospect of studying, remember this: *Committing yourself to learn is always an adventure of faith.* No one else can learn for you; the contest is between you and the subject you're studying. It is in the nature of learning that mastery comes with time. Einstein didn't discover the theory of relativity when he was in diapers. Probably he goofed up the first piece of arithmetic he did, just like the rest of us do. In other words, trust—in God and yourself—operates in the *long term*. (Incidentally, don't be *too* trusting of people on the other side of the lectern, since it is also in the nature of learning that nobody gets it right all the time.)

ORGANIZE. Study is basically a process of organizing facts and ideas. Therefore the skills that help you organize—skills of thinking, reading, evaluating, assimilating, and relating—are of prime importance. Cultivate efficient ways to record, memorize, and retrieve information.

If your impossibility is financial rather than academic, try turning your academic skill toward your practical problem. Keep focused on the vision you have for your education, and keep reinforcing your resolve in order to make the sacrifices necessary to realize your goal.

PERSIST. "If any of you lacks wisdom," writes James, "let him ask of God who gives to all liberally and without reproach, and it will be given him" (James 1:5). It is not stretching the text too far to suggest that part of the wisdom James is talking about has to do with education. Certainly, as with prayer, the rewards of study do not come immediately. They have to be worked for, unearthed, slowly amassed. But never lose heart. Persistence will get you there, and you'll find some pleasant surprises on the way.

Every now and then in the process of study come moments of enlightenment so dazzling and satisfying they make many hours of work worthwhile.

Consider the student who passed the Oxford University entrance exam with flying colors. One of the questions on the paper was "Write in not more than 2000 words a description of your own personality."

His answer?

"Concise."

GREAT RELATIONSHIPS

Angela was made to feel unloved by her parents. "You've got a negative attitude toward life," they said to her. "Nobody's going to want you if you're like that." Today she's overweight and doesn't take care of herself. She's lonely, yet she shuns company.

Mike would love company but he's unable to find it. He works in an office with men and women his own age; however, since he is a Christian and refuses on principle to drink alcohol, he has become something of a social outcast. Although he desperately wants to fall in love and get married, he has little opportunity to meet young Christian women. On top of this, he lacks confidence. He spends a lot of time in the evenings watching TV.

Carole is 30. She is a good-looking woman, but she was widowed three years ago and has been left to raise a pair of young children on her own. Working and looking after the children take up her whole day. She badly wants male companionship, but on the few occasions when she is able to go out she is treated with suspicion. Married women friends are suddenly protective of their husbands. Men back off as soon as she tells them she's a widow with children.

Relationships can hurt.

We've all known what it is to be in pain because we can't find friendship and love. We know, too, how easily obstructed our relationships become by moods. Jealousies, anxieties, and differences of background and values. Personal relationships should be a source of joy to us, yet it seems so hard to make them work.

This whole area of life is so fraught with problems and enigmas that you might think it better to stop trying to relate to other people and instead become a kind of Robinson Crusoe. But there aren't many of us who can be Robinson Crusoes and also be *happy*. However problematic our relationships become, we need them if we're going to enjoy life to the fullest. Singer Billie Holiday made the point with poignant clarity: "A person who don't have friends might as well be dead."

Long-Distance Dating?

Relating, then, is the only way forward. But how can you start a relationship and be sure, once you've started it, that it won't become unpleasant?

One increasingly popular solution is the personal column. Advertising yourself like a job vacancy has the twin advantage of screening the applicants before meeting them and of spelling out in precise detail the kind of relationship you're looking for.

Whatever enticements may be thrown into the deal, this method of relating has a major weakness: It concentrates on *compatibility*.

I'm not denying that this method could be helpful in sharing with your future friend or spouse a passion for collecting pink plastic flamingos. Common ground at least gets you talking. But I don't think the "impossibility" enters the scene at this particular point. People who find friendship and romance impossible will often make little headway even with someone who shares their interests and views. Getting conversation going is fine; the real problem comes in how you talk.

He, She, and It

In many ways, thinking of a relationship as a kind of object jointly owned by two people can be unrewarding.

Although we use the word for convenience, there is really no such thing as a "relationship"; there are only *individuals who relate*. When we say that a relationship is good, we mean we are relating well; when we call a relationship bad, we mean we are relating poorly.

The difference between the noun and verb is crucial. Someone who says that he "finds it hard to form a relationship" often thinks of the relationship as an "it" which he must bring into being. That's nonsense. A relationship exists *as soon as you meet another person*. The real question is not how you can establish a "relationship" but how you can behave in such a way that the other person is disposed to be friendly and loving toward you. How can you turn impossibilities into possibilities in your relationships?

Let's begin at the beginning. When two individuals meet, they nearly always take what you might call a "relational pose." In *The Great Gatsby*, Scott Fitzgerald gives a good feel of relational pose when he describes Gatsby's ill-fated introduction to the woman with whom he has been passionately in love for years. The woman, Daisy, is escorted into the room by the narrator, a mutual friend:

> We went in. To my overwhelming surprise the living room was deserted.
>
> "Well, that's funny," I exclaimed.
>
> "What's funny?"
>
> She turned her head as there was a light dignified knocking at the front door. I went out and opened it.
>
> Gatsby, pale as death, with his hands plunged like weights in his coat pockets, was standing in a puddle of water gazing tragically into my eyes.
>
> With his hands still in his coat pockets he stalked by me into the hall, turned sharply as if

> he were on a wire, and disappeared into the living room. It wasn't a bit funny. Aware of the loud beating of my own heart I pulled the door to against the rain.
>
> For half a minute there wasn't a sound. Then from the living room I heard a sort of choking murmur and part of a laugh, followed by Daisy's voice on a clear, artificial note:
>
> "I certainly am awfully glad to see you again."
>
> A pause; it endured horribly. . . .[1]

The relational pose accepted by Gatsby—one which involves acute and crippling embarrassment—gets the romance off to a disastrous start. But it also illustrates the fact that your relational pose (which, if it doesn't exist beforehand, usually takes shape in the initial moments of interaction) can make or break you in the quest for love.

There are three main types of relational pose which can best describe your own behavior.

A pose of *admiration* is adopted whenever one partner is "looked up to" by the other. The admired person is often more famous, more experienced, more wealthy, or more beautiful—or sometimes just older or more "together." Either way, the feeling of inequality is prominent, with the result that the admirer usually remains passive for fear of committing some social blunder.

It can be just as awkward on the other side. Most writers, for example, are uneasily aware of the celebrity status imposed on them as soon as they disclose their profession. But even if they enjoy the I've-always-wanted-to-meet-a-real-writer syndrome, they soon discover that admiration is no basis for a stable, long-term relationship—which is why, in the long run, being incredibly famous can also mean being incredibly lonely.

A second relational pose is *limitation*. If admiration results in massively unbalanced communication, limitation results in almost none at all. One person deliberately keeps the other at arm's length, not rudely, but establishing bounds beyond which intimacy will not be allowed to grow. He or she does not "get involved." Conversation stays at a superficial level and does not end with a warm invitation to "keep in touch"—unless it's clear from the tone of voice that this is a pleasantry and not a serious proposal.

The problem with both admiration and limitation is their tendency to demean the weaker partner. To suffer limitation is to be demeaned; to admire somebody in the sense defined above is to demean yourself. Neither side really engages with the other. Yet we know from experience how much there is to discover in another person; we know there's vast unanticipated wealth hidden—if only we will look for it. So what is the key?

It's a third relational pose, called *appreciation*. To appreciate people is to enjoy them by letting them be themselves. You can and should accord a person respect for being, let's say, one of the ten richest men in America; but don't embarrass him by acts of self-abasement, nor remain aloof on the grounds that a wealthy businessman isn't your type. Once you've met, your relationship will blossom or fade according to the way you choose to behave. As Jesus rightly said, "... with the same measure you use, it will be measured back to you" (Matthew 7:2).

If You Want a Friend, Be One

I have resolved to try to make a friend of everyone I meet, even if that friendship lasts only two minutes.

The laws governing good friend-making are the same whether you live with someone, work with him; or just exchange a quip or two while he rings up your groceries. In his excellent book *The Fine Art of Friendship*, Ted Engstrom gives ten rules for friendship which I've found especially helpful. I have summarized them as follows:

TEN WAYS TO FRIENDSHIP

1. DEMAND NOTHING. "We must decide to develop friendship in which we demand nothing in return." Being demanding—of time and tolerance—is one of the main reasons why some people fail to make friends. But, ironically, it is often by demanding nothing that we actually receive the most.

2. BE INTERESTED. "It takes a conscious effort to nurture an authentic interest in others." In other words, appreciation doesn't come easy. But if you give up at the start it won't come at all.

3. BE PATIENT. "Each of us is a one-of-a-kind creation." Therefore, it will always take time—often a long time—to understand one another. The same could be said of a country you move into. It takes time to learn the language and customs, and to drive on the left side of the road instead of the right. But learning brings familiarity, and familiarity brings enjoyment.

4. LISTEN. "Commit yourself to learning how to listen." It's a common mistake in communication to plan your own next witty remark when you should be listening to what the other person is saying. Don't you want people to listen to you?

5. BE AROUND. "Simply be there to care, whether you know exactly what to do or not." Often, as in a bereavement, there is no "right" thing to do except be on the scene. Your presence is a source of comfort, so be available.

6. DON'T ACT SUPERIOR. "Always treat others as equals." Paul instructs the Christian "not to think of himself more highly than he ought to think" (Romans 12:3). The reverse is also true. Equality is basic to appreciation.

7. PRAISE. "Be generous with legitimate praise and

encouragement." No one likes a sourpuss. Conversely, we all respond with almost childlike pleasure to sincere praise. The moral doesn't need spelling out, does it?

8. PUT FRIENDS FIRST. "Make your friends Number One, preferring them above yourself." If you give up an afternoon to help a friend decorate his apartment, you're telling him he matters to you. You're also likely to have a good time.

9. SEEK GOD'S FRIENDSHIP. "Learn to love God with all your heart, soul, mind, and strength. Then love your neighbor as yourself." It's in God's love for all mankind that we find the most powerful reason to love others. It's in God's love for us as individuals that we find the strength to love even when we don't feel like it.

10. BE POSITIVE. "Emphasize the strengths and virtues of others, not their sins and weaknesses." Nobody's perfect. That means that you can break a relationship down by finding faults, or build it up by ignoring them. Which is more important to you? The relationship or the faults?

I would make only one addition to Ted Engstrom's list, and that is *etiquette*. It may just be, for example, that the other guests at a dinner party raise an eyebrow or two when you dig into the spaghetti with your hands! Every social group has a few unspoken rules; come what may, you are expected to observe them. Failing to do so will not advance your quest for social integration.

An Unusual Love Story

They were a stunning couple—he a tall, blue-eyed, blond Dutchman and she a raven-haired Swiss beauty. They fell in love the moment they met outside Interlaken, Switzerland, in the summer of 1938.

Matthijs Vandenheuvel and Gilberte Sandoz were in their late teens, and their meeting was most improbable. War clouds hovered over Europe, and inter-European travel was slowing down. It was at this time that Matthijs' father, an important political figure in Holland, took his family on vacation in Switzerland. Gil, whose home was in French-speaking Geneva, was studying German in German-speaking Interlaken. Since Matthijs knew both French and German, it was easy for them to communicate. They didn't need to use the language of the literary classics to speak of their love for each other.

When they said goodbye at the end of the summer, they didn't know that they wouldn't meet again for seven years. But when she left with her parents, Matthijs felt their separation would last a long time. Though he wasn't a religious man, he went on his knees and prayed to see Gil again and that she might become his wife.

He had to wait.

With war breaking out in Europe, the probabilities of their meeting again were "impossible." Hitler invaded Holland, and Matthijs' older brother headed up the Dutch underground. The Gestapo was in possession of both of their pictures, and they lived constantly under the threat of arrest. If arrested, they would have been shot.

A few of Matthijs' and Gil's letters made it through the erratic mails, but they were so heavily censored that the remaining content was almost meaningless. Yet at least the letters let each lover know that the other was still alive and well.

In 1942, because of his unique position and connections, Matthijs had the opportunity to travel to Geneva. But his devotion to the struggle of his fatherland wouldn't let him go, though he passionately wanted to see his love. It wasn't until September of 1945 that Matthijs, through an arrangement made by his family, succeeded in getting a Dutch visa for Gil. She arrived in Holland on one of the first Swiss commercial planes to make the trip after the war.

In 1944 Matthijs invited the Lord Jesus to take over control of his life. It was 1953, seven years after their marriage, that Gil came to Christ. Since that time their Christian influence has been profound, both in Geneva and in Portugal, where Matthijs set up a highly successful business. They have been very conscious of the direct leading of the Lord through these years. Looking at them today, you know that nothing has changed in their feelings for each other. They show all the verve and dynamism of a young couple still enjoying their first love. And they are quick to give all the glory to God for His grace and faithfulness (Psalm 40:5).

Write Your Own Love Story

I would be misleading you if I suggested that love, like a toy train, can be wound up, released, then relied upon to run smoothly to the other end of the track. The greater part of love isn't something you feel or find or fall into—it's something you *do*.

This applies not only to sustaining love in a long-term marriage relationship but also to initiating the special kind of love which leads to marriage. You don't just hang around waiting for fate to write you into someone else's love story; you start writing the story yourself.

Impossible?

Don't you believe it! It doesn't matter how much you've been hurt in the past, or how much you may have failed or disappointed those you've tried to love. You can turn your impossibilities into possibilities if you're prepared to trust, organize, and persevere.

Of course, the story you write will be unique to you. You're the one who designs the plot, and you won't be wanting any detailed suggestions from me. Still, as you get down to the planning, let me offer you a few guidelines.

Before You Begin

There are not many authors who can sit down cold at the typewriter and start writing a book.

It's the same with relationships. You are going to be the main character in your story, so what kind of character are you? Start with a few basics: You're five-six, blonde with blue eyes, a cosmetics salesperson who likes Bogart movies and sumo wrestling (watching it). Is that the kind of character you envisage for the story? In what ways does your present character differ from the one you'd like to "write about"?

My guess is that you'll have a dream version of yourself that approximates some famous celebrity. That's fine, but it's not *you*. If you suddenly find yourself resembling Cher or Robert Redford you'll probably die of shock. What you need is not character *replacement* but character *development*.

Development builds on what already exists. There is a certain combination of gifts, looks, and personality that belongs exclusively to you and makes you a special person. Maybe you're not too thrilled with the ingredients, but don't worry—few of us are. If you're like most people, you won't have been using your unique resources to the best advantage. Much of your specialness is probably still vacuum-packed and stored away as potential. It needs to be unpacked and put to work.

At a simple level, this might mean a brush of lipstick or a visit to the hair stylist. But the more important developments involve your *behavior*. For instance, how are you doing with Ted Engstrom's ten principles of friendship? Are you consciously perfecting your conversation, making sure you don't come across as either a mouse or an overtalkative bore?

Are you trying to appreciate other people? Are you trying to enjoy life so that your arrival at a social gathering is like a window opening to a spring garden and not an incessant dripping of rain through a leaky roof?

Exactly what you develop in your character is up to you. Remember two things, though. One: Don't adopt some ridiculous role that has nothing to do with the person you really are. The name of the game is *improvement*, not acting. Two: The purpose of the exercise isn't to make you more impressive, but to make you more *likable*. Impressiveness may bring you admiration, but it won't bring you love.

Now sit down at that typewriter.

WRITING YOUR ROMANCE

1. THE INTRODUCTION. Sooner or later you're going to meet the other main character in your story. But where? Probably the best place to "set the scene" is a place to go for some form of relaxation. If you don't go anywhere, take up aerobics, volunteer work, racquetball, or chess—anything you're interested in that puts you in company with other people. One of the best places to meet someone is in church. But don't go specifically hunting for a date; just enjoy life, and let the story unfold.

2. THE OPENING CHAPTER. The two characters meet. Maybe your feelings are stronger at first than those of the other character. That's okay; remember that in the end the love story is a collaboration between two people. You can't write every scene the way you want to. But keep working on it; give complete freedom to your creativity. Scenes get repetitive if they're always set in the same park or restaurant, so use a little imagination with the setting. Throw in a few red roses and lakeside picnics.

3. THE SEX SCENE. Modern writers always make the same mistake with this one: They put it in too early. Shoving the characters in bed together before page 10 shows a serious misunderstanding of sexuality. Sex isn't an Olympic sport, something you can be "good

at" in an impersonal way. Sex is the ultimate form of *relating*. It is meant to be pleasurable, but the giving and receiving of pleasure are only a means of enhancing the relationship.

Jack Dominion in his book *Marriage, Faith and Love*, writes: "During sexual intercourse the couple reduce their boundaries until they fuse into one. This...oneness of coitus renews afresh trust, security and the sense of being recognized, wanted, and appreciated."[3] To use sex in a short-term or experimental relationship is to relate badly. The sex scene in the love story (written together by both characters) belongs on the final page. In the words of the Bible: "Therefore a man shall leave his father and his mother and be joined to his wife, and they shall become one flesh" (Genesis 2:24).

The TOP Lover

TRUST. Often the impossibility of relating well is rooted in a low self-image—an unwillingness to believe we can be loved. That unwillingness distorts the truth. Everyone *is* already loved by God; everyone *can* be loved by others; everyone *should* be obeying the commandments to "love the Lord your God with all your heart, with all your soul, with all your mind, and with all your strength" and to "love your neighbor as yourself" (Mark 12:30,31).

ORGANIZE. The secret of finding friendship is to be a friend; the secret of being loved is to love others. These are, to a large extent, ways of behaving that we can adopt or neglect as we choose. If we adopt these skills we have a chance to develop the potential within us so that we become not more *impressive* (in a way that merely draws admiration from others) but more *likable* (in a way that enhances the mutual appreciation necessary for a stable, long-term relationship).

PERSIST. There are ways of persisting in love that are not helpful. Take for example, the time when the man or woman you fell for married somebody else. However, in the building of relationships (that is, in relating well) generally persistence is essential. Friendship and love are both voyages of discovery. If Columbus needed persistence, so will we!

There is another and quite different reason for persisting in relationships. Persistence in this context is a virtue. It is called loyalty.

For instance, persistence indicates seriousness. Can there be any loyalty without persistence? Is not persistence the core of loyalty? Does not Jesus, Himself, say, "Continue ye in My love" (John 15:9 KJV)? Why? Because failure to "continue"—failure to persist—denies loyalty.

Impossibilities are not converted to possibilities through a fluke, but through persistence. A friend recently said to me, "Our era of the instant gratification syndrome robs us of life's greatest benefits because these come from persistence." Whether it's growing a garden, founding a business, developing a skill, or creating a meaningful relationship, persistence is the key.

4

A *HAPPY* *FAMILY*

A happy family? Impossible!

Today it's hardly a family at all. Dad gets out of the house just as quickly as he can after breakfast so he can keep paying the bills. Mom spends her day in a frenzy of cooking, washing, ironing, and buying groceries, serving supper in relays so she can drive Junior to the youth club before Junior's sister comes back from her dance class. Dad's late (as usual), but goes out after supper to fix the backyard fence, leaving Mom to load the dishwasher while Junior's sister and her friend play games involving flour and spoons in the freshly cleaned living room. Junior, when he comes back, goes straight upstairs to watch TV. Junior's sister has already been up longer than she's allowed and has to be forcibly bathed by Dad and put to bed. Junior follows at ten. Between ten and ten-thirty Mom and Dad sit over coffee in the kitchen with zombie-like expressions, mentally bracing themselves for the next day.

You don't need me to tell you that parenting is one of the toughest jobs around: screaming babies, sleepless nights, wrecked automobiles, shattered nerves. Somebody ought to pay you for it! It's no wonder that when Dr. James Dobson conducted what he calls a "Frustrations of Parenthood Poll," parents turned out to be less worried about their children than about themselves. Here are some of the anxieties that parents expressed in this poll:

- "Not knowing how to cope with children's problems."
- "Not being able to make the children feel secure and loved."
- "I've lost confidence in my ability to parent."
- "I've failed my children."
- "I'm not the example I should be."
- "Seeing my own bad habits and character traits in my children."
- "Inability to relate to my children."
- "Dealing with guilt when it seems that I have failed my sons."
- "Inability to cope."
- "It's too late to go back and do it right."
- "I'm overwhelmed by the responsibility of it all."[1]

Your Goal As a Parent

The impossibilities of parenthood vary with the age of your children. In addition, you may be saddled with other problems. Your child may be hyperactive or have some kind of disability or behavioral disorder. These problems amplify if you have been left to raise the family on your own.

Isn't it amazing how problems multiply? Harry, for example, had no particular difficulties with his children even while he was abusing drugs. Things started to go wrong only when he was diagnosed as being HIV (Human Immunodeficiency Viruses) positive—the precursor to getting AIDS. Soon after that his wife walked out on him. He was left weak, bereft, and in fear of the future, single-handedly caring for two small children who (predictably) were showing signs of emotional disturbance. Harry barely copes.

Parents' feelings in situations like these are often in turmoil. You feel helpless because things seem out of control. You feel guilty because other parents seem to manage when you don't. You feel exhausted because there's no time to relax and recover your strength. You keep on trudging round and round on this parental treadmill, but you never get anywhere.

What can you do?

One important priority is *trust in God*. He is always there when you need Him.

But although trust in God is essential, on the level of organization *you* are the one who acts as decision-maker and goal-setter. Whether you're into parenthood and finding it an impossible reality, or looking ahead to it as an impossible prospect, it's important to ask yourself what long-term goals you have in mind. The baby which your friends and relations spoil won't always be a baby. He or she will pass through childhood and adolescence to become an adult like you.

Picture yourself meeting with your future child as your own contemporary. What kind of person would you want him or her to be? You would probably like to be parent to someone who is kind, considerate, decisive, loyal, and honest. If that's your goal, what strategies can you devise that will help your child to turn out as this good, whole, and well-adjusted person? One strategy might be to give him or her "space." Let me explain what I mean.

Space-Making

As we grow older, the physical space within which we have a degree of privacy and freedom gradually increases. For example, the privacy which an infant enjoys is restricted to his crib. As he grows older, however, he's likely to be given his own room, and as time goes on he will be given unsupervised periods away from the home.

At maturity, the focus of his private space moves outside the home altogether.

Reflected in this development of physical freedom is a development of personal and psychological freedom. This is both the most necessary and the most difficult aspect of parenthood. Your son or daughter will need to become a responsible, independent person, just like you. But involved in that change is a breaking free from reliance on parental care.

Here too are stages:

1. Dependence
2. Counterdependence
3. Independence

You'll notice your children hitting Stage 2 around puberty. The telltale symptom is contrariness: Whatever view you take, your child will take the opposite. This can be very disconcerting. As parents, even Mary and Joseph did not understand when Jesus, quite properly, began to assert His independence:

> So, when they saw him, they were amazed; and His mother said to Him, "Son, why have you done this to us? Look, Your father and I have sought you anxiously." And He said to them, "Why is it that you sought Me? Did you not know that I must be about My Father's business?" But they did not understand the statement which He spoke to them. Then He went down with them and came to Nazareth, and was subject to them, but His mother kept all these things in her heart (Luke 2:48-51).

Life would be much easier for parents if every child's stage of counterdependence terminated in a vow of obedience! But that is an unreasonable demand to make of any ordinary child. Counterdependence, for all its trials, is a river that must be crossed if a child is to progress to full independence, and the art lies not in avoiding the crossing but in crossing well.

You can't cross the river on your child's behalf, but you can assist him by "making space" psychologically, just as you make space physically.

You need to make space for:

1. HORMONES. Adolescence is a period of intense biochemical change. The impact on emotions and behavior can be swift and distressing for parents. But there's nothing unusual about a child becoming moody at this time of life—in fact, it would be unusual if it didn't happen. Be prepared for it.

2. PERSONALITY. Two highly organized parents I know could never understand why their teenage son left his room in a mess. "You're just being sloppy," they said. "If you're going to graduate, you'll have to get your life in order." They unwittingly drove him to the brink of a nervous breakdown because they didn't understand that he had a personality which was fundamentally different from theirs. To them, untidiness of mind and habit indicated confusion; to him it was the outward sign of inward order. That doesn't mean, of course, that messiness should be encouraged. But make space for a growing mind to organize itself as it needs to.

3. PEERS. It's important that young people feel secure and accepted in their peer group. Their peers are the generation to which they belong and within which they are developing a new and different sense of being "at home." If adolescence is a "breaking out," there must be something good to break into.

4. CULTURE. The next generation is not your generation, but it's the one your child will be living in.

Attitudes such as "I didn't do it that way" will rarely be constructive. You may hate modern music, think that most teen idols are lazy, good-for-nothing slobs, and deplore your children's taste in clothes. But you're not the one who has to make friends at their high school, are you? So make space!

Positive Intervention

You may call "space-making" an abdication of parental duty.

If parenting consisted only of giving freedom to children, you'd be right. Of course there's another side to the story. Peers can be a bad influence, and certain aspects of contemporary culture are undoubtedly evil. A child needs protection as well as liberty.

The question is, How can I give protection effectively? Doesn't it quickly boil down to sanctions and confrontations and a breakdown of communication? As Ogden Nash observed:

> A child need not be very clever
> To learn that "Later, dear" means "Never."

It's often said that the best way to make a teenager disobey you is to give him orders. There's truth in that statement. The stage of counterdependency may look like a challenge to parental authority, but in many ways it is a demand for reassurance and love. If you start to argue when your teenage daughter defends her choice of boyfriend, you are in fact reinforcing your role as "a grown-up who doesn't understand" and diminishing your role as "the parent who loves." The "grown-up who doesn't understand" relinquishes the right to advise; the loving parent keeps the lines of communication open so that *when the young person asks for it*, good advice can be given.

I have a close friend, a minister to thousands, whose daughter at the age of 19 was dating a young man of whom my friend and his wife did not approve. However, instead of "preaching" at his daughter, he prayed for her and gently advised her when she brought up the subject.

At one o'clock one morning he and his wife were a bit disturbed that the young man was still at the house. But they preferred his being there than at some place of questionable activities.

As my friend was dropping off to sleep, his daughter came in, shook him gently, and said, "Daddy, Bill wants to know how he can become a Christian. He wants to turn his life over to Jesus. Will you come in and help me explain it to him?"

Though she did not marry the young man, the time they spent together ended in a most profitable way and in a most wholesome friendship.

The loving parent will also be careful to ensure, as far as possible, that at each stage of development the child has outlets for spare energy and a positive peer-group environment. Decisions on this are usually made at an early stage. Some parents, for example, have deliberately chosen to live in more remote country areas, or have joined churches with lively youth programs, so that conditions are favorable for raising children. That way there is some hope of avoiding too great a chasm between the values of the family and the values which the children pick up as members of their own generation.

Parenting actually has two aims. One is to establish the child as a mature, independent person. But the other is to maintain the child's place within the family. The best way to keep the child "on your team" is to make sure your "team" is the kind the child wants to be part of. Most children, especially in the adolescent stage, will test parental parameters. They will argue with mom and dad about parental restraints. That's part of growing up. But if he knows he is loved and has positive experiences of family life, he will want to identify himself in the family as well as in his own peer group.

Like Father, Like Son

Attorney Robert C. Field suffered the trauma of the Georgia State Bar Examination twice. The exam lasts 2½ days and requires a solid three months of cramming if you're going to have a hope of getting through. When he took the exam in 1958, the average success rate was about 25 to 28 percent. He passed the first time.

In 1984 his son Jeff took the same exam. Bob Field had been careful to maintain a good relationship with his son, and when it came to exam time he was careful with his encouragement.

"It's not going to be a pushover, Jeff."

"You think I'll make it?"

"I think you've got a sound educational foundation, and as far as I'm concerned that gives you a good chance of passing the first time with flying colors."

He placed a hand on his son's shoulder. "But I don't want you to worry if you fail. You're an intelligent young man. Your mom and I believe in you."

"I don't know if I could bear to go through it all twice."

"I know. But remember, you get what you work for in life. Sometimes it takes persistence."

Jeff nodded. "Well, I'm not going to fail."

"Good. That's the spirit."

The results took three months to come through. Participants were notified in two ways: first by a list of names posted in the county courthouse, and second, a day later, by mail. Bob prayed that God would give his son peace with the results. When the day came, Jeff went to the courthouse to see the results. He was on the phone to his father when the list went up. His father heard the following dialogue:

Jeff: "Is my name on the list?"

Voice: "I don't know. I'll take another look."
(pause) "No, your name's not on the list."
Jeff: "Dad, it's not there. I didn't pass."

Bob's heart dropped into his stomach. He felt terrible for Jeff, but at the same time relieved, because he could hear Jeff congratulating his friends. Before the day was over, Jeff was already planning his study schedule for the next exam.

As anticipated, the letter confirming the result arrived the following morning. Since Jeff was out, it sat for most of the day on the den table. Finally, walking past it for the twentieth time and curious to find out how bad the bad news was, his father decided to open it. It began: "We are happy to inform you..."

What a cruel way to break the news that Jeff had failed!

"...that you made a passing grade on the State Bar Examination. However, we cannot certify your status until we receive a certified copy of your law school records."

That was why the result hadn't been posted in the courthouse! Jeff was phoned immediately. He couldn't believe it. In 24 hours he had gone from the doldrums of failure to the ecstasy of success. "Who knows?" wrote his father afterward, "Maybe the Lord wanted Jeff to experience this as an object lesson, to build character and help him handle problems in the future."

Whose Hands on the Wheel?

There are three things that children seem particularly averse to doing. Eating (the right food at the right time), going to bed (when you want them to), and doing schoolwork (of any kind, on any occasion). If you're facing impossibilities in these areas, you're not alone!

From the children's point of view, the issue is usually "It's mean of you to make me do what I don't want to."

From the parents' view (unless they are extremely liberal), it's "You don't understand now why we're doing this to you, but one day you will. So in the meantime...."

Discipline—it's the sharp edge between intervention and space-making. There's little doubt that discipline is essential for a child's development. But how much to apply, and in what way, is a matter of some sensitivity. The easiest approaches (because they require the least effort) are censorship and laissez-faire—either subduing children by force or letting them run all over you. The most difficult, but also the most effective, is a degree of discipline that makes it clear who's boss without having to call in the Marines.

Here are two pieces of sound advice.

First, establish your bottom lines, and stick to them consistently. If you tell your child you're not going to come upstairs *again* because he or she wants a drink of water, don't go back on your word.

Second, never impose discipline (especially not punishment) without making it clear to the child that he is loved. Discipline isn't just there for your convenience as a parent—it's for the good of the children.

Help!

One of the most solidly knit family units I've ever known is the George Barbar family in Boca Raton, Florida. When one of George's sons was in his 20's, unmarried, completely mobile, and quite wealthy, he still lived at home. That's the Lebanese tradition.

If he told his father he would be in at 11 o'clock and found he could not be there at that time, he would stop wherever he was and phone his father, telling him what time he would be in.

One day a friend of the family said, "George, it's amazing how your children are so close to you and Alice. I notice that your boys report to you the moment they come in; they put their arms around you and kiss you. It touches me deeply. My 18-year-old daughter has been a source of great heartache and anguish to me. How can I get her to have the same relationship with her mother and me that your children have with you and Alice?"

George replied, "You're 18 years too late."

Parenting can go wrong. It's not uncommon for children to "go off the rails" to such an extent that parental authority breaks down. There are many reasons for this, but when a child gets stuck at the counterdependence stage and starts letting out all that spare emotional energy in aggression, roles in the family undergo a drastic reversal. Suddenly it's the teenager who's in charge.

The situation was summarized by columnist Ann Landers in a 1981 article in *Family Circle*:

> So what can parents do with kids who have them backed against the wall?... Heaven knows reasoning, pleading, crying, threatening, and bribing hasn't worked.

Her solution:

> You must find the courage to withdraw your money, influence, affection, anger, guilt, and pleas that he or she learn to shape up. You must begin to make real demands entailing severe consequences. You must make it clear that you will not live in a house with people who mistreat you and do not respect the rules you have laid down. You do not need your teenager's approval. You're the boss. The sooner your youngster understands this, the better.[2]

Providing support for this kind of action is an organization called Toughlove. Its philosophy is summarized in the name. You are not rejecting your child, but providing love in the only way it can now be useful. In effect this means imposing on a teenager a degree of discipline more appropriate to a five- or six-year-old. That's significant, because research shows that in most cases of parent-battering, the teenager never had that kind of discipline earlier on. Introducing it now might save the situation. If not, it will at least make your life easier as a parent.

(Toughlove has over 1500 groups across the U.S.A. and Canada. If you're interested you can contact the head office at the Community Service Foundation, P.O. Box 70, Sellersville, Pennsylvania 18960.)

The TOP Parent

TRUST. Becoming a parent is a step of faith. You are committing yourself to at least 20 years of determined effort in a job for which you may get precious little thanks. That's hard. Yet having a family is undeniably a blessing. So there is a sense in which your parenthood is a vocation—something God has called you to, and for which He will give you the strength and wisdom you need.

ORGANIZE. As a parent-to-be, you will probably have resolved to give your children the best possible start in life. That's excellent. But don't make the mistake of thinking that the "best" is located someplace between a parent's generosity and a child's desires. The best start you can give your children is a good environment—a good mix of "soil" where character and spirit can grow. Organization is vital. Prepare yourself by reading widely. *Make space* for these new human beings to develop and establish their independence. Structure your family life to secure *positive intervention* where it is needed. Use *discipline* wisely and firmly. Remember: No matter how wild the child, it's never too late to become a better parent.

PERSIST. One benefit of good organization is that it reduces pressure on parents. Still, 20 years is a long time. Over those two decades the particular challenges you face will change with the age of your children and the social conditions under which you live. Be aware of these complexities, and be ready to respond.

Augustine, later to be known as Saint Augustine, was a dissolute young man. His mother, Monica, prayed for his conversion. She died while he was still giving play to all of his hedonistic impulses.

After his conversion at 36 years of age, he freely acknowledged that it was the persistent prayers of his godly mother that brought him to Christ and thus to an honorable life-style.

A young friend of mine, now 29 years old, abandoned the parental values and teachings of his parents when he left for school. He even experimented with drugs. His mother and father never ceased loving him, gently counseling him, and praying for him. They didn't preach at him. In a few years, he experienced a 180-degree turn in his life. Today he is a dedicated young businessman, happily married and father to a daughter whom he is rearing "in the nurture and admonition of the Lord." His parents never gave up. They persisted.

5

IMPOSSIBLE MARRIAGE?

Dr. Hugh Musof and his wife know what it is to go through the hell of marriage breakdown.

Hugh was born into a Brooklyn Jewish family. As a young man he stepped into a society with materialistic values.

He met his bride-to-be in 1965. They fell in love and got married. But married life wasn't what they had expected. Some marriages dissolve after ten or twenty years, but the Musofs' marriage fell apart in only three. When they separated, Hugh's wife was going through a nervous breakdown.

Hugh considered his options. His friends' advice was simple: "Divorce her. You made a mistake. It didn't work out. There are no children. Your practice isn't off the ground yet. Get out and start a new life."

Divorce certainly seemed the easiest solution. But just as Hugh was ready to file, his wife turned to God. Because of that, the whole tenor of their relationship changed. Her experience with God had made her a genuinely new person, and Hugh, after much heart-searching, decided to stay with her.

It wasn't easy repairing the hurts that had built up over the early years of marriage. From one point of view, new difficulties emerged because of Hugh's background as a Jew. For a long time, life was mediocre and unfulfilling. It was in 1973, to find out if they could enrich their relationship, that the Musofs agreed to go on a Catholic Marriage Encounter weekend. That didn't end their problems, but it did help the two to sort them out. For the first time, Hugh was encouraged to confront some of the issues in himself that had contributed to the breakdown of the marriage.

He finally gave his life to the Lord in 1977. That, of course, isn't the end of the story. In a way there's no such thing as "the end of the story" in any kind of marriage. The Musofs have continued to work at their relationship, and gradually it has given them more and more joy and satisfaction. Through trust, organization, and persistence they have established a lasting and fulfilling marriage.

Married and Miserable?

In my previous work as a church pastor I've seen a lot of marital misery. Here are a few sample cases that may chime in with your experience:

- A wife who hardly ever sees her husband because he works long hours and socializes with his friends on weekends. She resents being left to look after the kids and feels taken for granted. Because the wife is forced to perform both parental duties, it becomes increasingly hard for the husband to fill his natural place in the family when he's home. Tension forces them apart.

- A husband who has lost his job and his role as breadwinner. He loafs around the house, bored and irritable, getting in the way. His wife complains to him. Arguments mount over money, holidays, the children. Home life becomes claustrophobic and bad-tempered.

- A couple who can't relate sexually. He wants sex five or six times a week. She wants to be

romanced. Neither feels satisfied. He seeks
sexual fulfillment outside the marriage; she
finds another man who "understands her"
and she eventually leaves her husband, taking the children with her.

Impossible marriage situations like these are extremely
common. Sometimes they're contained by the good
humor and tolerance of the partners, but sometimes they
open huge chasms between husband and wife that neither feels able to bridge. Either way involves much pain
and suffering.

If your marriage is going through a rough time, you're
not alone. *Every* marriage has its tensions—even the
ones that look perfect from the outside. And this isn't
just because moral standards have sunk over the last few
decades, or because modern men and women are somehow less capable of surviving long-term marriage than
their parents or grandparents. Marriage itself is *changing*.

It's been changing gradually in the West for 50 years.
The older pattern of marriage emphasized aspects clearly
visible from the outside—social respectability, fidelity,
children. By and large, husbands and wives didn't stop to
wonder how they related. That's the crucial change,
because husbands and wives today are likely to see their
relationship as the substance of the marriage. The difference is explained by psychiatrist Jack Dominion:

> . . . this movement from external to internal
> reality, expressed in the realization of the po-
> tential of feelings, emotions and sexuality in a
> relationship of equality of worth, is the con-
> temporary ideal. Its realization varies from
> couple to couple, but there is not the slightest
> doubt that it is affronts against these aspira-
> tions that ultimately press people to terminate
> their marriage.[1]

This is a vital clue to the weakness of modern marriage. Many other factors are at work behind America's notorious 50 percent divorce rate. But for two reasons the new model of marriage is more fragile than the old one.

First, it is in a constant state of *flux*. If the purposes of marriage are to establish a home and raise children, it is comparatively easy for the partners to feel they have achieved their goal. However, if the purposes are internal—that is, focusing on mutual fulfillment and satisfaction—the scene is constantly and subtly shifting.

The husband at 40 is not quite the same man that his wife fell in love with when he was 25; nor is she the same woman. Time changes them—changing their roles, their attitudes, their bodies, their needs, their desires, their abilities. If they are each to remain fulfilled and satisfied, they will have to work hard to ensure that they change in harmony.

But here they face the second reason for fragility: Marriage, like any relationship, is *complex*. It works on combinations of levels, and can deteriorate—slightly or seriously—in a great variety of ways. How a partner feels about his or her work, parenthood, finances, status, security, and sex (to name only a few areas) all affect the stability of the marriage. And—as anyone will know who has argued with a spouse about money—you can't disturb one without throwing the rest into disarray.

Deal with the Stress Points

Breakdown in marriage begins with pressure at the *stress points*. Broadly, these fall into six groups:

1. Control of *cash*
2. Divison of *labor*
3. Use of *leisure*
4. Stabilizing of *emotions*

5. Sharing of *sex*
6. Accommodation of *change*

Some stress points come with the territory. There aren't many couples, for example, who haven't at some time disagreed about major life changes in employment, housing, and children. Others crop up randomly, depending on the couple and their situation.

However, the presence of stress points in a marriage doesn't in itself make the marriage a bad one. All marriages have such stress points, and the damage they cause frequently varies in proportion to the pressure exerted—which is why divorce is associated with external circumstances like unemployment, debt, and house-moving. What makes a marriage good is not *the absence of stress* but *the ability of the partners to recognize stress and defuse it*.

The process of defusing stress is like removing bilge water from a boat—it ensures that stress does not accumulate to a level where it endangers stability. But defusing stress is not easy because *points of stress are almost always points of weakness*.

John and Jane have a typical rocky marriage. The main stress point lies in Jane's feeling of being neglected by her husband. John is aware of her feelings, but because he is unwilling to confront his own inability to express love he justifies his behavior by saying that Jane is "stiff" and "unapproachable." There is some truth here. Because she lacks personal confidence, Jane needs more affirmation than her husband is able to give her. She interprets his shyness as rejection, and this further undermines her confidence and renders her less able to take the initiative in showing affection.

It's easy to attribute John and Jane's problem to lack of communication, but it goes deeper than that. To address the stress point honestly, each would have to admit to the other a weakness that he or she prefers to keep private.

Consequently, each blames the other for causing the breakdown. Fear of touching the raw nerve of personal weakness prevents them from defusing the stress and restoring their marriage to wholeness and joy.

They Make Marriage Work

A real "John and Jane" known to me (for obvious reasons, I cannot supply their names) prove that a pressurized marriage can be successful.

She was a stunning beauty, a Miss America in terms of her looks, talent, and social grace. He was the proverbial tall, dark, and handsome man with a keen mind and an acumen that commanded the attention of the business community before he was 40 years old. When the two of them walked into the lobby of a hotel, heads turned. Yet their marriage was a series of holocausts, and eventually they divorced.

But neither was happy. I don't know if she dated other men. He was seen in the company of other women, but found no satisfaction. John and Jane longed for each other. When they finally met again for serious discussion, top on the agenda was the possibility of remarriage. But before they went ahead they made a number of resolutions:

1. Neither one would trash the other verbally.

2. Neither one would deceive the other.

3. Everything in their relationship would be "on the table," without rancor or hostility.

4. She would be in such a position financially that at any time she wanted to she could walk out.

5. They would not "hold in" feelings relating to each other's behavior.

6. She would become a full partner in the area of philanthropy. It would be she who signed the checks.

7. If their views were unalterably opposed, they would agree to disagree and drop the subject from discussion.

On that basis they remarried.

There were no miracles. But they placed their trust in God, and they organized to maintain a fulfilling marital relationship. And it's working. Although they still have major differences of opinion, they are able to subordinate those differences to the higher goal of rebuilding their marriage. Trust, organization, and perseverance are paying off. Every time I am with them, I leave with the conviction that they reciprocate a profound love built on a solid, unshakable foundation.

The Twofold Way of Marital Happiness

That couple is using the first of two practical solutions to transform an impossible marriage:

ONE: Extend the contract.

The exchanging of vows is integral to a wedding service. In the old Anglican form, bride and groom promise to maintain their marriage "for better for worse, for richer for poorer, in sickness and in health, to love and to cherish, till death us do part, according to God's holy ordinance. . . ."

This is, in effect, a contract—a set of rules that both parties solemnly agree to keep. But it is a *general* contract with a universal application, and so it is drawn up in the most basic of terms.

If they wish to, however, there is nothing to stop them writing in extra roles later on. They don't need to get married again in order to do it; they don't even have to ratify the new commitments in a formal public setting (although it may help them if they do). What they *do* need to do is think out the implications: first, whether a given rule will defuse a given stress point, and second, whether they are willing to regard that rule as binding. Only if both these conditions are fulfilled can the rule help them.

You may feel this approach to be constricting. In a way it is; but it constricts in order to liberate. The husband in the last section made a sacrifice when he gave his wife control over their philanthropy. Yet in doing that he affirmed his trust in her, and so allowed her to become more fully herself and more able to contribute to the marriage.

Remember, too, that contracts don't have to be agreed to bilaterally. You can resolve, without telling your partner, to adjust your behavior in a way that reduces stress and increases time for growth. Ted Engstrom tells a good story about a man who hated his wife so much that, before he filed for divorce, he consulted a psychiatrist just to find out how he could make life miserable for her. The psychiatrist listened carefully before he replied: "I think I've got the perfect solution for you. Starting tonight when you get home I want you to treat your wife as if she were a goddess. I want you to change your attitude toward her 180 degrees. Do everything in your power to please her. Listen intently to her when she talks about her problems, help around the house, take her out to dinner on weekends. I want you to literally pretend that she's a queen. After two months of this wonderful behavior, just pick up your bags and leave. That should get to her!"

Joe thought this was a great idea. Life in his house changed overnight. He brought his wife breakfast in bed. He sent her flowers. They went on two romantic weekend vacations. They read to each other at night. Two months later the psychiatrist called up:

"Joe," he asked, "how's it going? Did you file for divorce? Are you a happy bachelor again?"

"Divorce?" Joe asked in dismay. "Are you kidding? I'm married to a goddess. I've never been happier in my life!"[2]

TWO: Positively reinforce.

In Luke 6:38 Jesus gives some advice that people with marriage problems will do well to think about:

> Give, and it will be given to you: good measure, pressed down, shaken together, and running over, will be put into your bosom. For with the same measure that you use, it will be measured back to you.

Marriage survives on *giving*, for giving is the essence and the final expression of love. When marriage starts to go wrong, however, giving is the first trait to be abandoned. There sets in, instead, a stalemate of "I'll stop hurting you if you start being nice to me." Each partner waits for the other to make the first move.

That kind of position is dangerous because negative responses become the norm. Interaction follows little pre-set programs. The husband comes home; the wife, expecting a bout of temper, treats him coolly; noticing this, the husband is irked and asks what's going on; an argument flares; the wife says "I told you so!" and walks out. To preserve integrity, each partner needs to prove the other wrong, with the result that the worst expectations are fulfilled on both sides.

Fortunately, this process can be reversed.

The secret is *positive reinforcement*—giving encouraging signals back when the other person does something you like, and as far as possible turning the other cheek when he or she does the reverse. In part, this works just because human beings are suckers for praise. But husbands and wives are also tied more securely than they think. Usually there lies, not far below the surface, a powerful desire in each partner to be loved by the other, with the result that even in the middle of a fight, it's possible for old feelings to be suddenly and violently rekindled.

I'm not recommending manipulation or transparent insincerity. It's just a fact that a gesture of appreciation for behavior you like in your spouse will usually encourage him or her to behave that way more often.

Did you compliment your wife the last time she put on a new outfit? Did you tell your husband how much you enjoyed spending yesterday evening with him at home?

Positive reinforcement counts!

Can Marriage Fail?

I'd be kidding you if I said there was no such thing as an impossible marriage. In some marriages the partners are, for whatever reason, so ill-matched that real happiness is out of the question. One partner may have betrayed the other through infidelity, or both may have lost beyond recall the commitment needed for marriage to work.

Yet the escape-hatch solution to marital breakdown is being overused to the point where commitment in marriage is losing its force. Serial polygamy is more than a phenomenon—it's a norm. For example, Melvin Belli, author of *Divorcing*, seems to regard divorce as a lifestyle: "It's all right if you're a four-time repeater like me," he says, "because eventually you'll get the message about how to improve your life if you are motivated to do so." Yet Belli is currently going through his fifth divorce at 81 years of age.

If your marriage is beyond repair, but you don't want to divorce, it is both possible and honoring to God to exercise "damage control."

The Agony of Divorce

Here is Marcia's moving story. I asked her to write it out for me. It speaks for itself eloquently.

> The yellow-and-blue pills were laid out on the dresser in the bedroom. There must have been 100 of them, "more than enough to do the job," I moaned to myself. As I paced the floor, all I could think of was stopping the excruciating pain I felt. I thought of my four children. What of *their* pain on finding Mommy's lifeless body on the floor? And, of course, there was God. What would He think? Even in my agitated condition, I knew I could not go through with it. Replacing the pills in the bottle, I angrily spat out the word that had gotten me into this mess: *divorce*!
>
> This was supposed to happen to other people. My husband of 19 years had just declared he was leaving me. Even now it seemed impossible. This wasn't in the plan. After all, we were missionaries. Didn't that automatically protect us from horrors such as this? In our small, conservative community, divorce was never an option.
>
> My mind darted from one thought to another like a bee trying to light on a flower. Did people live through divorce? Would God still love me? Could I continue to serve Him? Would my church reject me? What would happen to my children? I was in a dark tunnel with no light at the end.
>
> With my emotions on a roller coaster and depression hovering like a vulture, I tried to consider my options. The choices seemed bleak. Slowly, painfully, I took inventory of my life.

Years ago, as a young Jewish woman of 16, I made a decision to follow my Messiah. I had given Him all I had: my life. Suffering the painful rejection of my family, I went far away to a Christian school. There I met and married a man who also wanted to serve God. What had gone wrong? Was God no longer in control of my life? I desperately needed to know.

Over the next weeks and months I read and reread the Scriptures. At first I tried to find loopholes which would vindicate me and get me off the hook so I would not need to forgive anyone. Wasn't I, after all, the *dumpee*? Wasn't I the "innocent" party? The Holy Spirit began His tough work inside me. My anger turned to reason; reason to acceptance. I knew I had nowhere to go but to God, and that He required total obedience to His principles— no picking and choosing on my part. I reasoned to myself, "This is a monumental opportunity for God to do His thing." There would be no turning back. What a relief to have that settled!

Now to apply these truths to my daily life. At first all I could do was trust God for an hour or two. Then I was able to say, "Get me through the morning." When I could go an entire day trusting Him to control my life, I thought I had climbed to the summit of Mount Everest! Praise would become a lifeline to God, not just an occasional choice or an afterthought. I began to see order coming out of chaos. Maybe we would make it after all.

These decisions began to define not only *my* life but the lives of my children. My confidence in God and dependence on Him were the stability we needed. The car wouldn't start: Pray! The radiators banged in the night, signalling no heat in 20-below weather: Pray! My 13-year-old son broke his elbow, and we were in the hospital alone and afraid: Pray! My 19-year-old was told he had cancer, and when waves of despair threatened to overwhelm us, we prayed and trusted God's plan.

Of course, one doesn't always trust God's plan. I turned 40 and was divorced the same week. It felt as if I had been run over by a Mack truck. I cried myself to sleep that night. It wasn't the first time, and it wouldn't be the last. The realization of assuming the day-to-day development of four children, meeting their physical, emotional, and spiritual needs, was too much. I was desperately afraid. Since my mind would run wild at times and so often it was difficult to concentrate even enough to read the Bible, I found that listening to tapes of Scripture or of the singing of Psalms had a very soothing effect.

"The goblins will get you if you don't watch out." This familiar line from childhood proved true. Yes, there were goblins. Some of my goblins were feelings of rejection and worthlessness, loneliness, feeling trapped, bitterness and anger, feeling as though others controlled my life, feeling as though I had a contagious disease, etc., etc. Rejection is knowing that your husband has chosen someone else. It's sleeping in a double bed—alone. Loneliness is sitting in church and singing some of the same hymns that were played at our wedding. Or seeing your daughter play her violin and knowing that her daddy is 3000 miles away and would never share these times again. Anger is sitting in the back pew at church looking at all the couples together and saying to yourself, "I'd be a better wife to _____ than his wife," and mentally killing her off!

The children and I collaborated on a major change: One son decided he would live with his dad in California and go to college there. The three other children and I moved from the house in which we had lived for 18 years and from the small community in the Midwest to Atlanta, closer to my birthplace. Even though we all made this choice, it wasn't easy. Our family was splitting up, causing us untold grief. The second son was struggling with whether or not he should go to California to be with his brother and father after his junior year in high school. I told God I didn't think I could bear this, and I knew that my youngest son would desperately miss his big brother. But I suggested to my son that he counsel with a close friend of his at church and that I would give my unqualified support to his decision. He chose to stay!

I was learning about life. I learned that I must hold my children with an open hand. They are not possessions; they belong to God. I made a decision to preserve, at all cost, their relationship with their father. I refused to allow them to be in the middle. What if this meant they would *all* go to live with him? I would leave that in God's hands.

Looking back now, years later and with all four children following after God, we can see how He protected and provided, how time and again He confirmed His love to us and rewarded obedience.

Ask me now if I can face anything with God, and my answer is ABSOLUTELY! I know that life's most difficult circumstance is not beyond His control. Without a shadow of doubt, when I reach the future, God is already there.

Happily Ever After—Again?

During an early pastorate I met a young woman of such quiet but surpassing devotion to Christ that she has come to mind for 40 years whenever the topic of dedication comes up.

I never saw her piqued, depressed, or sullen. Her radiant face, always wreathed in a smile, bespoke tranquility and peace. She could be found at church every time the doors were open. She taught Sunday school class. She sang in the choir. She carried a full-time executive position. She reared her daughter, three years old when I first met them. She did all this without once seeming hurried or anxious.

Yet her marriage had been incredibly painful.

From the time she was a little girl, her desire was to be a missionary on a foreign field. In her late teens she met a handsome young man who announced he was studying for the ministry. He seemed to possess all the qualities a Christian young lady would want in a husband. They were married.

At that time he was in the military, which meant they were apart for long periods. On one occasion she joined him in Atlanta for rest and recreation. It wasn't a long visit, and after a too-brief time together he told her he would have to leave immediately. They said goodbye. But when she reached the bus station, she realized she had left something at the hotel. Only minutes after they parted she came back to the room they had stayed in. Her husband was in bed with another woman.

When she first discussed the situation with me, she was in her mid-twenties, and the divorce had already been finalized. I volunteered that she had scriptural grounds to remarry, but she opted not to. She was dating nobody, was interested in nobody. She simply wanted to raise her child in the best possible environment.

She maintained her radiant, faithful life and service. Twenty-five years later her daughter said to me, "Dr. Haggai, I am so happy in my marriage. I wish my mother could have that same happiness. Would you see anything wrong in that?"

I said, "In 1949 I told your mother that she certainly had grounds to remarry, but she opted to devote herself to you."

The conversation stirred me deeply. I was glad to hear a short time later that a godly and well-respected widower had taken an interest in the lady, who was by then 50 years old. They married, and for 15 years their home has been the center of a rich influence for God. Delay is not denial. This lady maintained an unshakable trust in God, organized her life in a way compatible with that trust, and persisted in patience for a quarter of a century until God blessed her with an idyllic marriage.

The TOP Marriage

TRUST. Trust lies at the very heart of marriage. Husband and wife receive each other's vow in the expectation that it will be kept. If your marriage is in trouble, you may feel that your partner has let you down. That may be true, but a successful marriage relationship is built on a *triangle* of trust—between you, your spouse, and God. Most problem marriages feature a decline of trust on all sides. To rebuild the relationship, you must cultivate not only your trust in your spouse, but your spouse's trust in you, and most of all your joint trust in God.

ORGANIZE. Trust goes hand in hand with *commitment*. That's not a popular word today, but the fact is that no marriage can be saved without it. Both partners must want to preserve and improve their relationship before effective action can be taken. There is no shame involved in consulting a marriage counselor—after all, marriage is highly complex, and somebody else's guidance can be valuable. But there are many other options open to you as well. Two particularly helpful ones are *extending your marriage contract* (agreeing to abide by particular rules to relieve pressure on marital stress points) and *positively reinforcing* behavior you like in your spouse by giving praise, encouragement, and love. Remember that although you and your partner are changing, the person you loved enough to marry is still there. Thinking about the way you communicate can help set the "original" person free.

PERSIST. A marriage relationship is like a house-plant. If you tend it, it will flourish; if you neglect it, it will wither and die. You *must* persist in tending your marriage, because everybody must persist. It's the name of the game. But this doesn't mean that life turns into a wearisome round of forced politeness. You want things to improve, and you want to reawaken love. So does your spouse. The tending may always be necessary, but if you persist it won't always be an effort. The day will come when you say "I love you" just because you want to.

6

Dynamic *Leadership*

Marcia didn't ask to be made leader of her family. It was forced on her by her husband's divorce after 19 years of marriage. Suddenly she was in sole charge of her four children. She wondered how on earth she was going to cope.

Guy landed a top-ranking job that took him to the top of his department. He was used to working alongside people, but he had little experience in long-term leadership. When the phone call came telling him he had been given the job, he got cold feet.

Lisa is a single woman who worships at a Presbyterian church. She's loyal but shy. Not long ago the minister decided it was time that Lisa was offered a position of leadership in the congregation, and he asked her to take charge of a young women's group. She was panic-stricken.

Marcia, Guy, and Lisa are three people who have done a double-take at the prospect of leadership. All three have proven to be excellent leaders, but none of them dreamed they were capable of handling the kind of leadership position they now occupy. Like many people, they doubted their ability to lead.

Me a Leader?

You may think good leadership is impossible for you. You may think, "Leaders are born, not made."

Are they?

Moses, who surely must count as one of the world's most successful leaders, initially showed all the signs of becoming a first-class wimp. True, he killed an Egyptian for beating a Hebrew slave, but after this act of protest against Egyptian tyranny he promptly retreated to the desert. If God had let him, no doubt Moses would have stayed there for the rest of his life.

Moses had to be forced to recognize his true calling, and even then it was a struggle. When God announced that He was about to send Moses to Pharaoh to demand freedom for the Israelites, Moses cast around desperately for excuses. Who, he pointed out, was he going to say had sent him? And why on earth should Pharaoh take any notice? God pressed His point patiently:

> But Moses said to the Lord, "Oh, my Lord, I am not eloquent, either heretofore or since thou hast spoken to thy servant; but I am slow of speech and of tongue." Then the Lord said to him, "Who has made man's mouth? Who makes him dumb, or deaf, or seeing, or blind? Is it not I, the Lord? Now therefore go, and I will be with your mouth and teach you what you shall speak." But he said, "Oh, my Lord, send, I pray, some other person" (Exodus 4:10-13, RSV).

This isn't the Moses we imagine turning Nile waters to blood and filling Pharoah's bedroom with frogs. Nor is it the Moses that artists have depicted brandishing his staff before the Red Sea and breaking the tables of the law as he descends from Sinai to find the Israelites worshiping the golden calf. If Moses finished his career as a powerful and charismatic leader, he certainly didn't start it that way. In fact he didn't want to be a leader at all.

Moses belongs to a large class of people who have made an impact on society *in spite of their apparent weakness.*

Demosthenes had such a serious speech impediment that he was embarrassed to speak in public. The thought of his becoming a communicator in ancient Greece was crazier than snow falling in June. But Demosthenes learned the skill anyway. He shaved one side of his head so he wouldn't be tempted to socialize, then practiced relentlessly by the sea until he overcame his problem. He became the father of Western oratory.

My late brother Ted decided to become an electrical engineer even though his college aptitude tests put him at the bottom of his class in math. His teachers advised him to pick another field, but he refused. Day after day he worked to develop the necessary skill. He lost 30 pounds. But by his third year at college Ted was tutoring in math and graduated with honors. He later won the L.A. Hyland award for scientific achievement.

In 1980 the *Harvard Business Review* collected 15 articles on leadership under the title *Paths Toward Personal Progress*. The gist was that even though some people have more natural ability than others, leadership itself is a learned skill, just like surgery or management. In other words, leaders are made, not born. Consequently, as Ivan W. Fitzwater points out in his excellent book *You Can Be a Powerful Leader*, the real difference between leaders and nonleaders is one of *attitude*. You can rise above innate aptitude.

Leadership is not an impossibility for you. With commitment, hard work, and trust in God, you can turn the impossible to the possible.

Attitude not Altitude

When little Ed was ten years old, his parents were divorced. Then each remarried two years later. He had to decide if this was a loss or a gain. He was a precocious fifth-grader. He determined to make a choice. He could benefit, based on his values, outlook, and faith. Or he could feel sorry for himself. He decided that he was blessed, not deprived, since he had twice the normal number of parents, grandparents, homes to go to, birthday presents, Christmas presents, sources of advice and counsel, fishing partners, family friends, people to love, people to love him, letters to receive, homecomings, homegoings. He then began to feel sorry for his friends who had one-half as much as he did.

Read his own words: "This experience was the first time I realized that faith, attitude, and outlook can overcome events, traumas, things, and the actions of others. Subsequently, after becoming a pilot, I was again reminded that the difference between fear of crashing on the earth, fear of going into outer space, and enjoying the flight is attitude, not altitude. God is always my Co-pilot, and He loves to fly."

He wrote this to me when he was 40,000 feet over Greenland on a flight from London to Seattle.

Ed Stanley turned the impossible into a positive benefit. If anybody had been asked whether ten-year-old Ed Stanley would become one of the nation's celebrated businessmen, the answer would probably have been, "Impossible." Yet, in less than 35 years, he was the president of the Young Presidents Organization International.

Today he is chairman of the Management Compensation Group, NW, Inc. (MCG). It's a national financial consulting firm doing executive benefit planning and funding for Fortune 500 companies. MCG is made up of professionals, including actuaries, attorneys, CPAs, investment bankers, insurance consultants, and benefits specialists.

Stanley is also chairman of the Stanley Investment and Management, Inc. (SIAM). SIAM engages in international barter and counter trade programs and international business brokerage.

He is chairman of Fine Arts Graphics, Inc., a company specializing in corporate letterheads, business cards, and stationery items for large national corporations throughout the United States.

He is trustee of Lewis and Clark College, Saint Vincent Medical Foundation, and the Oregon Symphony.

He is director of the GPG plc, a London-based holding company for American and European financial services firms, traded on the London Stock Exchange. He is director of GMCC, a New York-based subsidiary of GPG plc.

He is director of Aspen Airways (United Express) Inc.

He is honorary Counsul General of the Kingdom of Thailand.

He is a former member of the Oregon Economic Development Commission.

He holds an MBA in marketing and finance from the Harvard Graduate School of Business Administration.

He was decorated Commander of the Most Noble Order of the Crown of Thailand.

He is on the Board of Governors, Museum of Flying, Santa Monica, California. He is a multiengine, instrument- and jet-rated pilot. He is former chairman of the State of Oregon Aeronautics Commission.

What Is Leadership?

Ed Stanley's story demonstrates the truth that a determination to lead is God's guarantee you can do it.

But what images do you have in mind when you use the word "lead"? How do you see yourself in your future role as a leader? If the position is a prominent one, you will probably be tempted to attach to leadership some of the same features that popular culture attaches to it—glamour, toughness, power, wealth. You will see yourself as respected by your enemies, admired by your friends, and obeyed by your followers. You will, in short, want to savor the benefits of leadership before counting its costs.

I don't want to cool your ardor, but I do want you to understand what leadership is really about. W.C.H. Prentice said in the *Harvard Business Review* in 1961: "Attempts to analyze leadership tend to fail because the would-be analyst misconceives his task. He usually does not study leadership at all. Instead he studies popularity, power, showmanship, or wisdom in long-range planning." Taking my cue from Prentice, I use the following definition:

> Leadership is the discipline of exerting special influence within a group to move it toward permanent beneficial goals that fulfill the group's real needs.

This has three implications for you as a potential leader. *First*, leadership is not the same as dominance. You don't force others to do what you want—you *motivate* them. *Second*, you operate in the context of a group—a collection of individuals who share certain characteristics or interest and whose cohesion depends on unity of purpose. It is the ability to mobilize unity (often by visualizing goals invisible to others) which sets you apart as the leader. *Third*, the goals you aim for must be high-quality goals. They must establish changes that are both beneficial and permanent, and enhance the future welfare of the group.

The importance of the definition is clear if you remember what happens to leadership once the restraints have been removed. Lead by domination and you create the conditions for domestic violence, boardroom bullying, and political dictatorship. Fail to forge unity of purpose in the group and you forfeit your right to lead, whether as a church group coordinator or as head of a sales team. Set goals that are malevolent or provisional and you become either a moral renegade or an ineffectual trifler.

The 12 Principles of Leadership

In my book *Lead On!* I identified 12 principles that make leadership possible:

VISION:
: A clear picture of what the leader sees his group being or doing; the driving force behind leadership.

GOAL-SETTING:
: A set of specific, measurable steps that design the program for fulfilling the vision.

LOVE:
: The outgoing of the totality of one's being in beneficence and help; an act of the will; the "fruit of the Spirit."

HUMILITY:
: Love's mood; the lowliness that pervades the leader's consciousness as he contemplates God; freedom from pride or arrogance; submission to others, helpful, courteous. Humility has no self-consciousness.

SELF-CONTROL:
: Love's mastery; a way of life by which the leader rules his spirit and does not let his desires master his life; temperate in all things.

COMMUNICATION:
: Presenting worthy thoughts worthily; the means by which a leader informs, impresses, convinces, entertains or actuates; the leader's most valuable asset in transferring truth through speech and writing.

INVESTMENT: A principle that says if you invest or give something, you will receive it back many times again.

OPPORTUNITY: Cleverly disguised as obstacles or seeming insurmountable problems; a principle that turns blunders into benefits.

ENERGY: Conveys ideas of authority, excitement, success, and purposeful vitality; demonstrated through physical vitality, mental alertness, hard work, commitment, perseverance, attention to detail.

STAYING POWER: A principle that says problems and difficulties can be overcome through perseverance, persistence, or "hanging on"; overcomes a host of impossibilities such as financial limitations, illness, family opposition, betrayal, persecution, misunderstanding.

AUTHORITY: A principle that recognizes the distinction between internal and external authority and says a leader should enhance internal authority; a conviction that the leader can move the people in his group toward goals of beneficial permanence.

AWARENESS: A principle that calls the
                      leader to be aware of all
                      elements that contribute to
                      excellent performance, his
                      leadership role, the meaning
                      of leadership, and all the
                      preceding principles of
                      leadership.

Figure 6.1 represents these principles in diagrammatic form. Although the principles overlap, they can also be divided into three groups on the basis of orientation. ACTION calls primarily on the leader's ability to maintain vision, set goals, invest time, and capitalize on failure. RELATION demands qualities that get the best from others—love, humility, communication skill, and authority. SELF is a leader's inner bearing that rests on self-control, endurance, vitality, and awareness. Figure 6.1 shows the three orientations bound together in a way that defies the senses but which at the same time suggests dynamism and strength.

Leadership As ACTION

In 1964, when I was in the ministry of evangelism, I made a visit to West Asia. The experience jolted me, because I met Christian leaders who told me that the age of traditional Western-led missions was drawing to a close. They were right; I could see with my own eyes that the indigenous churches had developed to a point where Western missions—admirable though it was—had become outdated in the same way as colonialism.

Believe me, nobody could have been more surprised than I! But a fire had ignited in my soul. When we reached the Indonesian island of Bali, I told my three traveling companions that I would be dropping out of circulation for a while. I shut myself in my room and

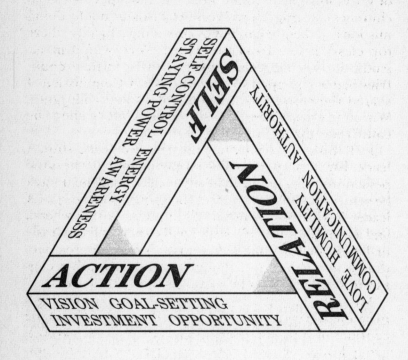

Figure 6.1: The 12 Principles of Leadership

reflected. In that solitude, a vision—a surge of fresh, exciting ideas—came to me so fast that I had barely written one thought down before the next flashed into my mind.

What I wrote down remains to this day my philosophy of world missions. From it grew the concept of Western churches assisting Third World Christians, not by doing missions on their behalf but by providing a facility where top-class leaders from the Third World could meet, study, and exchange insights, returning to their countries better equipped to obey the Great Commission. I shared the vision with trusted friends and colleagues. Within five years Haggai Institute (as it later came to be called) was up and running.

I tell this story to illustrate the nature of leadership. A leader isn't just a person with stripes on his cuff; he is the person who sees better than anyone else what goal must be achieved, and then enables the group to achieve it. A leader in title only is nothing more than a figurehead, and a group with such a leader will either drift aimlessly or be led by someone else whose vision and creativity draw others to him even though he is not officially recognized. Leadership, in other words, demands *vision*.

My vision happened to take me outside existing organizational structures. Yours may be contained within the confines of your job description, your position as youth group leader, or your natural leadership within the family. But whether you lead as a mother or a CEO, your practical effectiveness depends on how well you can serve those around you by channeling their energies and capabilities toward a positive purpose.

Leadership As RELATION

If vision is the fundamental element in leadership as ACTION, its counterpart in leadership as RELATION is *love*.

This statement might seem strange to anyone for whom leadership goes hand in hand with power struggles on the board of management. Isn't it frankly a bit contradictory (or even hypocritical) to talk about love when the name of the game is really competition and survival? When the chips are down, can leadership always be motivated by love even in the home or at church, let alone in such aggressive environments as banking and big business?

The answer to these questions brings us face-to-face with the paradox of leadership as taught in the Bible. Nowhere in the New Testament do we find any approval for the power concept of leadership. Jesus is perfectly clear that—

> ... whoever desires to become great among you shall be your servant. And whoever of you desires to be first shall be slave of all (Mark 10:43,44).

As the ultimate leader, Jesus "made Himself of no reputation, taking the form of a servant" (Philippians 2:7), thus laying down a pattern of leadership for His disciples which is totally at odds with the one commonly practiced in the secular world. In order to lead effectively, He says, you must regard yourself, in relation to your group, as a servant. Most mothers will relate to that! But even leaders of multinational corporations will see immediately in Jesus' words the close link in leadership between love and humility. It's a combination that is fatal to the ego but great for group cooperation.

In 1970 I was privileged to spend three weeks with Dr. Han Kyung Chik, leader of the Young Nak Church in Seoul, Korea. I asked one of the men who worked with him how Dr. Han handled criticism.

"One time a session member made what to me was a savage attack on Dr. Han's judgment. Dr. Han wept. He said, 'Apparently I did not pray sufficiently before taking this course of action. Forgive me. I shall pray more earnestly about this.' "

"What happened?"

"Within a year the entire session saw the wisdom of Dr. Han's proposal and adopted it, even though he never again brought it up."

I can't think of a more powerful demonstration of love, or of the effect of love, in the policy-making of a large organization. By quoting the above I don't mean to recommend that you burst into tears next time somebody disagrees with you at a board meeting. It's the *principle* you need to internalize: that a good leader, far from browbeating his associates, gives and receives creative ideas in such a way that every individual is affirmed and the group is enabled to move forward in harmony.

In the home, that is the difference between slapping down (or ignoring) a child's suggestion and saying, "Well, Son, that's a great idea. Are you sure it's the right thing to do in this situation?" Discussion makes people feel valued, and in the end it makes them more creative and cooperative. It's one secret of making good leadership possible.

Leadership As SELF

Let me tell you about two men I once knew.

The first, Clifford Bron, was one of the greatest orators America has ever seen. When he spoke to a packed Miami auditorium in 1945, Dr. E.M. Dodd, minister of the prestigious First Baptist Church of Shreveport, Louisiana, introduced him to the assembled religious leaders and intellectuals as "the greatest preacher since the apostle Paul." That same year President Pat Neff of Baylor University ordered the bells switched off as Bron addressed the students for two hours and fifteen minutes on the subject of "Christ and the Philosopher's Stone."

Audiences everywhere were spellbound. At age 25 Clifford Bron had touched more lives, influenced more leaders, and set more attendance records than any clergyman his age in American history.

The other man was Dawson Trotman. Trotman was bright, artistic, and highly articulate. He was an exhorter, a man who always responded passionately to a challenge and who never feared making enemies. At age 27, with only one year of seminary and one year of Bible school behind him, he set up the Navigators, an evangelistic organization that stresses total commitment to Christ. He wasn't without his detractors. He suffered vicious verbal attacks but carried on anyway, fully believing the promise "Great peace have those who love Your law, and nothing causes them to stumble."

Both Bron and Trotman died before their time. Bron was in his mid-thirties; Trotman was in his early fifties. But they died in strikingly different circumstances. Trotman drowned while attempting to save a girl's life at Schroon Lake, New York. He left behind him an organization that ministers powerfully worldwide with a staff of more than 2500 people.

Toppled from leadership by drinking and fiscal shabbiness, and separated from his wife and children, Bron died in a third-rate motel on the western edge of Amarillo, Texas. He left nothing.

What distinguished the two men is the fundamental element of leadership as SELF—self-control. I don't mean just working hard; I mean maintaining a firm discipline in every area of life and in every waking hour. Here again, popular images of the successful leader (like the TV soap executives who apparently can say no to anything but sex) give a misleading version of the truth. Private follies carry a public cost to the leader, as presidential candidates know only too well. Any leader who indulges his weakness—for sex, alcohol, or dishonesty— is taking an enormous risk with his credibility.

On the other side of the coin is the fact that leadership itself demands a controlled lifestyle. No one gets to the top by leaving the office early on Friday afternoons or turning up late for appointments. But even this constitutes a serious problem for many people. So how can you develop self-control?

Dawson Trotman was on the right track. If he is to succeed, a leader must build not only his SELF, but also his RELATION and ACTION, around his spirituality—a regular program of prayer, meditation, and study of the Scriptures. That discipline is, so to speak, the largest tree in the forest. But it should be supported and reinforced by other disciplines as well: the discipline of regular exercise; the discipline of scheduling and planning; the discipline of guarding thought and restraining speech. One discipline on its own may be uprooted in the first storm, but disciplines standing together give mutual protection and provide shelter under which sound leadership can be exercised.

The TOP Leader

TRUST. Leadership should be looked upon as neither an impossible burden nor a personal accomplishment—another item on an impressive resumé. Instead, it is a *responsibility which you hold in trust from others and ultimately from God.* When you assume a leader's role, you need to trust both in your own ability to master the skill of leadership and in God's willingness to help you fulfill your responsibility capably.

ORGANIZE. The 12 principles of leadership can be divided into three categories: ACTION (those principles concerned with the leader's role as visionary and goal-setter), RELATION (those principles concerned with the leader's place as group coordinator and motivator), and SELF (those principles concerned with the leader's personal efficiency and integrity). Successful preparation for leadership consists of comprehending and internalizing these principles.

PERSIST. The late Cecil B. Day—founder of the Days Inn motel chain—had only one wall picture in his original office. It showed a cat clinging desperately to a chinning bar. The words beneath read: "Hang in there, Baby." Cecil Day knew that good leadership didn't come easy.

I know this too, for I have made several near-disastrous blunders in my time, and though I felt wounded after they happened I can see now that they widened by experience and made me a better leader. So whether your leadership is exercised in the home, the church, or the world of business, *don't give up*. Learn leadership as you would learn to play the piano, and don't worry if it costs you time and effort. Just aim for mastery of the calling.

7

PERSONAL FULFILLMENT

If you could somehow get a copy of *The Washington Post* delivered to heaven the day after you died, what would you like to see written in your obituary?

I'm not talking about doubling your income by this time next year. I mean the nagging desire you have to achieve something that may be quite unrelated to your work or your marriage or your education or whatever else makes up your day-to-day life—the impetuous goal you've hardly dared mention to anyone else in case they laugh at you.

Draft an opening sentence. "Joe Spencer (1960-2055) decided at the age of 32 to become a high-altitude mountaineer...." "Margaret Howison (1942-2028), though accomplished in the field of international law, is probably better known to the public as a tireless fund-raiser for international aid...." Or maybe you prefer: "Franklin Schulte (1944-2031) will long be remembered for his scale model of Manhattan built out of empty cola cans...."

It doesn't matter how crazy it is. It doesn't matter whether it's a private passion or a special calling you feel you've been given by God. The ambition belongs to you. And this means that only *you* can work it out.

So are you just going to sit there and dream? Or are you going to turn the impossible into the possible?

An Impossible Dream?

From childhood Bodie Thoene dreamed of being a writer. But she realized even as early as kindergarten that she faced problems. The teacher would put each child's name on a slip of paper, then pile the slips on a table for the children to collect in order to claim their milk and cookies. Bodie always arranged to be last in line because she couldn't even recognize her own name.

After struggling at school for a few years she came home, at age eight, with "F's" on her report card. Her mother couldn't believe it because she knew how hard Bodie had worked.

"You don't deserve that," she said.

She pushed the report into her husband's hand. "You go talk to this teacher, because I'm going to be really, really angry if I talk to her."

Bodie's father took her to school. The teacher was firm in her assessment of Bodie's problem.

"She's lazy. She isn't even trying."

Bodie was devastated.

Her father listened politely, but on the way back home he put his arms around her.

"I know you're trying, aren't you?" he said.

Yes, she was. But the fact remained that Bodie couldn't read or write. Ask her to read "phony" and she would sound out "po" or "oph."

The interview had only compounded Bodie's feelings of guilt. It was a little while after this that she visited the Methodist church where the family went occasionally, and knelt at the altar in the basement. She didn't know it was an altar; except for the cross, it was covered up. But she had a deep awareness of God's presence there, and she prayed something like this: "Hey, You up there, I would like to be able to read and be like the other kids, and if You would help that to happen, I will do anything You want me to do with my life."

That very week Bodie's mother hired a special teacher named Nita Martin to come in every morning of the week and help Bodie to read, not by phonics but by recognizing the shape of the words. Nita acted words out—like getting up on a chair to illustrate fear of a mouse. By the end of the summer Bodie could read—not brilliantly, but well enough to get her through her schooling.

Her reading problem, though, yielded some surprising benefits. For a start, it gave Bodie a fascination with words. Her mother read to her so much that she picked up by instinct the rhythms that go into good writing. Because she read by listening, she also developed an extremely good ear for dialect, a gift which has stood her in good stead as a novelist.

It wasn't until Bodie flunked English in her freshman year at college that her problem was finally recognized as dyslexia. But by then she was already a published writer, having begun a column for a newspaper in Bakersfield, California, at age 14. God had turned her impossible ambition into a possibility.

While yet in her twenties, she achieved fame as a Hollywood scriptwriter.

Hollywood actor John Wayne wrote, "She [Bodie Thoene] has a talent for capturing the people and the times."

Bodie's literary skill so impressed Wayne that he asked her to write his autobiography. His family and friends were so delighted with her writing that they (Wayne Enterprises) kept her on for three years after his death.

Though she was now well-established as a writer, the haunting memory of her promise to the Lord as a girl kept nagging her, so she did a 180-degree turn and decided to write for the Lord.

She had told John Wayne that she wanted to do a story about Israel as it was in 1948. He thought it was a good idea. This desire grew stronger and stronger. Her mind was focused on the establishment of the State of Israel largely because it was through learning that so much prophecy was fulfilled in 1948 that she became a Christian.

She was just winding up her work with Wayne Enterprises. As you might suspect in Hollywood its normal for writers to bounce from one project to another. They rarely stay any one place. "Okay," she thought, "I'm about done here. What am I going to do now?"

She prayed about it. She had hardly begun praying when a producer phoned her to do some work; he wanted to discuss the possibility of Bodie doing a script about Israel in 1948.

She drove over to meet him. The first thing he did was pull out a book with the story of the British moving out of Jerusalem on May 14, 1948.

The producer told her the dramatic story: He described the bagpipes playing as all the soldiers marched out. The captain of the guard holds in his hand a key. It is the key to the gates of Zion. He goes to the door of the mayor of the old city of Jerusalem and knocks. When the mayor comes out, the captain says, "This is the first time that your people in 2000 years have been so privileged as to hold the key to the city of Jerusalem."

He hands this key to the mayor.

The producer told Bodie he needed a script in three weeks. Since it was to be a historical piece, a mountain of research had to precede the writing. It was to be a 60-page script.

"Three weeks? Sir, that's about a six-month job," replied Bodie.

"I know it is, but it's something that we just need to have done."

"Do you believe in miracles?" Bodie asked.

"Indeed, I do."

"Okay. I will attempt this impossible job."

All the time Bodie was thinking, "Well, here I am; I wanted to do a story about this subject all this time, and here I am sitting across the desk from a producer who wants me to do it. Maybe the Lord can come through on this."

"May I take the book that has this wonderful story in it?" Bodie asked.

"No, it's a library book. You can't have it."

So Bodie headed immediately to the North Campus Research Library of UCLA, where she does a lot of research work. However, she got into the wrong lane of traffic and ended up on Fairfax Street in the Jewish district of Los Angeles.

"This is terrible," she thought. "I'm half an hour away from where I'm supposed to be, and I'm lost—on Fairfax Street."

Bodie looked up and there was a Jewish bookstore. She got out of the car and went inside. "Maybe they'll have the book I want," she thought.

A Jewish lady and her husband waited behind the counter. Bodie asked for the book, and they had it in stock! "Boy, this is great!" she thought. "Maybe the Lord has some reason for my getting lost over here on Fairfax Street."

She purchased the book and looking over her shoulder as she headed out, she said, "What I really need is to talk to somebody who was in Jerusalem in 1948."

"My husband was there," the lady replied. "As a matter of fact, my husband's uncle is in that book you're holding."

"Oh, yeah? Who is your uncle?"

The man replied, "My uncle is Mordecai Weingarten. He was the mayor of the old city of Jerusalem, who took the key from the British when they evacuated in 1948."

Now this was only 20 minutes after Bodie accepted a job that should have taken six months! Within one hour she was in contact with the people in Jerusalem who had seen it all happen, who had been there.

Bodie says that this experience really changed her life. She ended up doing the script, but nothing ever came of it; it was not produced. So she forgot it for two or three years.

Then one night she thought about it and concluded that the Lord surely had some reason for giving her that experience on that particular day. In reflecting on that episode she caught the idea of writing a fiction series totally different from any movie. The series is known as *The Zion Chronicles*—a five-book series with 3000 manuscript pages. She did it in three years.

She is now a bestselling writer of Christian novels.

"Sometimes when you think things are impossible," said Bodie, "the Lord opens the doors."

Trust, organization, and *persistence* brought Bodie through. Note that they brought her through against impossible odds. What dyslexic child could seriously expect to become a successful novelist? She could have lamented, "Fate has denied me the opportunity, so I'll bury the dream." But she didn't; she persisted and succeeded.

Sweating and Groaning

The Roman poet Horace gives ambitious people some handy advice:

> The man who wishes to achieve a longed-for victory in a race must have trained long and hard, have sweated and groaned, and abstained from wine and women.

It's worth pondering. First of all, Horace reminds his readers that *ambition must be clearly defined*. There's a world of difference between saying you want "victory in a race" and saying that you want to "do some running." Vagueness moves you no closer to accomplishment; it's like sending a letter addressed to "G.M. Brown, California."

What do you want to do? Break the international record for women's 8000 meters? Take part in the New York Fun Run? Jog for half an hour each morning?

Whatever the ambition is, *name it specifically*. It's the only way you can measure your progress, or even know where you're going.

Second, says Horace, understand that *ambition demands sacrifice*. If you want to win a race you have a whole lot of sweating and groaning to do before you reach the track. And this principle applies to every ambition; there are, as General Eisenhower said, "no victories at bargain prices." Whether you're aiming to finish the marathon in less than $3\frac{1}{2}$ hours or to open your own art gallery, you'll be paying up front.

This doesn't mean, though, that you won't need your brains. What links ambition to achievement is a well-conceived and rigorously executed *goal program*. I mentioned Paul Meyer's SMART system in chapter 1 (SMART, remember, stands for *specific, measurable, attainable, realistic,* and *tangible*); now it's time to make a few more comments about goal-setting.

Think Backward

An ambition is like a destination: You know where you want to get to; what you don't know is *how to get there*. You need to devise a "route" made up of short-term or medium-term goals that will guide you toward your long-term goal or objective.

One master of this kind of navigation is Hei Arita, president of the Success Motivation Institute's subsidiary PJM Japan. Hei Arita is an extraordinary man, with extraordinary vision. This is an excerpt from a letter I recently received from him:

> Now I am challenging a new enterprise that most people think impossible. That is winning the World Cup Soccer Tournament.
> This started from my encounter with a man named Katsuyoshi Kuwabara. He was formerly the manager of Honda Soccer Team, and had a

dream of having a soccer team that could win the World Cup.

I was moved by his enthusiasm, and proposed to him that we actually challenge this goal. We set the year for 2002 and started looking for players. We organized a local soccer team, PJM Futures, and planned a soccer school for children aimed at supplying young soccer players in 2002. But we did not have a ground. We prayed to God and tried vigorously to find a suitable site to construct a soccer ground—then, soon after, we could find a place fitted for the soccer school.

Within one year we found a good location. We constructed a turf-covered ground, with an observation stand for audiences of 3000 and a club house. On top of this, I built a new office building nearby costing 500 million yen in 1988.

Notice how Hei Arita constructs his route backward from his destination. As soon as he has identified a goal he asks himself what preconditions will be needed to realize it. Obviously, if you're going to win the World Cup Soccer Tournament, you need a team. Any team? No—it has to be a first-class team, specially trained, so good that it's virtually unbeatable. How do you get a team like that? One solution might have been to spend a lot of money buying players from abroad; but that's no use, since a national team for the World Cup has to be made up of nationals. So Hei Arita goes for another solution: He sets up a soccer school to teach the kids who will be the right age to compete for the World Cup in 2002. That's a heavy investment, not least because the school will need a soccer ground. The first goal, then, becomes the acquisition of land.

Property development might seem a long way from

international success in sport. Nevertheless, logic makes
it the first step to that objective. The formation of PJM
Futures is almost incidental to Hei Arita's World Cup
ambitions, but he has another objective in mind for
them:

> Most of the PJM Futures have been baptized
> as Christians, and I wish to make this team a
> top-ranking soccer team in Japan, composed
> of Christian players. Then the National Soccer
> Ground would be the place of evangelism, and
> more Japanese would become Christian.
> All these things were said to be impossible by
> other people, but I believed in the possibility
> and kept praying to God. I had faith in the
> power of God.

In addition, Hei Arita has a confidence in his players
that would leave most team managers breathless:

> PJM Futures won all the 24 official league
> matches in the past 2 years, and are scheduled
> to keep winning for the next five years without
> any defeat.

Talk about turning impossibilities into possibilities!

Routes and Roads

In Hei Arita's plan for route-building, each goal is
deduced from the one that will eventually follow it by
asking the question: *What previous goal will I need to
achieve before this next one becomes feasible?*

So far so good. But the difficulty with goals is often not
one of mere recognition. If you have the ambition of
building a model of Manhattan out of empty cola cans,
it's not hard to identify "get two million cans" as a preceding goal. The real teaser is where you get them from.

To extend the previous analogy, it's easy to say that in order to reach a given destination you must pass through a given set of places; it may be harder to actually move from one place to the next. There are *roads* to choose as well as *routes*.

C. Burke Day, Jr.—son of the Days Inns founder—is someone who faced exactly this problem. Forced by a health problem to leave the construction industry, he searched for a new ambition in life:

> Somehow I had to find a way of making a living sitting down.
> That's how I started—by sitting down.

He decided, with the encouragement of friends and family, to try writing. His first goal was to get some articles published. But getting into print confronted him with new impossibilities.

> I tried selling true stories, like one when I was robbed in Switzerland and pushed out of a moving train. Rejected. Then, the story of how I ran back into my high school sweetheart and married her. Rejected. Desperate, I thought of fabricating a story of my secret romance with Minnie Mouse, but feared that it would be published and subject me to a libel suit. . . .

C. Burke Day, Jr., was hitting a breakdown on the road to his first goal. As it happens, this was the moment we had lunch together and I was able to refer him to my friend and Christian author Dr. John McCollister. That relationship has become a key factor in his progress toward publication. Today, Burke's articles have been published in *The Saturday Evening Post*; his new book—*Day by Day*—will soon be on bookstore shelves.

Taking the right "road" to a goal requires careful

GOAL:

Consultation	
1	
2	
3	
4	

Equipment	
1	
2	
3	
4	

Clearance	
1	
2	
3	
4	

Manpower	
1	
2	
3	
4	

Figure 7.1: Outline for Goal Inputs

thought. Yet this is a vital stage in overcoming the impossible. This time the question to ask is: *From where I am right now, what resources will I need to achieve this goal?* To stimulate your thinking, you may find it helpful to use an outline like the one in Figure 7.1. This covers four major areas of input in goal-achievement.

GOAL INPUTS

CONSULTATION: Any form of information, advice, or training from other people. This could consist of a few well-placed phone calls or even a college course.

EQUIPMENT: Hardware, software, clothing, premises, a car, a musical instrument. Any article you need to obtain before you can achieve your goal.

CLEARANCE: Is your activity going to cause inconvenience to others— family, friends, employer, neighbor, local administration, police? Does it require someone else's permission before you can begin? If so, make sure you get all the necessary clearances.

MANPOWER: If you're learning Mark's Gospel by heart, the only manpower involved will be your own. For wider goals, you may need a team of people to get the job done— perhaps even your bank manager.

Get It Right!

A curious story was carried in January 7, 1989, by the British *Independent* newspaper.

It concerns one Mr. Egidio de Luca, who had recently been transferred from a pleasant post in the Italian Foreign Ministry to become Deputy Director of Rebibbia Prison—a high-security center near Rome for terrorists and Mafia criminals. Evidently he hated his new job so much that leaving the prison service became his overriding ambition. He started plotting a way out.

His break came with the news that the Red Brigades, an old left-wing terrorist group, had established a new cell. After all, what more likely target could there be for an assassination attempt than a senior prison officer?

One weekday evening Mr. de Luca went with his bodyguard to a deserted street near his home, where he instructed the bodyguard to shoot him in the leg. When the police arrived, Mr. de Luca, lying in a pool of blood but still conscious, told them he had been attacked by three gunman claiming to belong to the "New Red Brigades," but that his quick-thinking bodyguard had scared them off before they could kill him.

Looked at in terms of goal-setting, Mr. de Luca's plan was a classic. The objective was to transfer from the prison, and the preceding goal was to persuade the police that an attempt had been made on Mr. de Luca's life. Unfortunately though, Mr. de Luca overlooked one thing. In the briefcase he was carrying at the time of the shooting, the police discovered Red Brigades literature which the victim had intended, but forgotten, to scatter around the scene for added effect.

At this point the real Red Brigades obligingly phoned from Naples to make clear that they were not involved. The authorities questioned the hospitalized Mr. de Luca, and the truth came out. He was charged with "simulating a crime" and of being "in unlawful possession of a weapon in a public place."

You can guess the moral!

The TOP Achiever

TRUST. Paul J. Meyer insists that goals should be *realistic*. In other words, it's no use aiming to become an astronaut when you're like me, in your sixties and just a tiny bit overweight. But don't let caution restrict your vision: Most ambitions aren't impossible. To have an ambition is to already have the inner drive which, with the right management, can push an idea into reality. Don't forget that ambition is often given by God. When the Lord said to Noah, "Make yourself an ark" (Genesis 6:14), He was laying down a pattern for human response to divine initiative. What is it that God has entrusted you to "make"? Do you think that if He has given you the ambition He will withhold the means to see that ambition realized?

ORGANIZE. Achievement in career, sport, arts, or any other area rests on your ability to conceive and implement a goals program. Start with your final objective and work backward, identifying at each step the goal which is required to make the next step possible. In this way you will build a *route* between yourself and your objective. When the route is complete, pay attention to the *roads*—the means by which each goal will be successfully attained. If it helps you, use the fourfold scheme of *consultation, equipment, clearance*, and *manpower*.

PERSIST. In one of the biblical parables, the unjust judge says of a persistent widow, "Though I do not fear God nor regard man, yet because this widow troubles me I will avenge her, lest by her continual coming she weary me" (Luke 18:4,5). It is the persistent who win.

A few years ago I had the privilege of meeting Australia's premier religious media photojournalist, Ramon

Williams. Ramon is as fine an example of persistence as I can call to mind. He sums up the wisdom of persistence concisely: "By now I've learned that 'no seats on the plane' simply means 'try the same problem from a different angle.' "

Go and do likewise!

8

EXPANDED INCOME

If I asked you to name a financial goal, what would you say?

- A 25 percent rise in income?
- A job paying 25,000 dollars a year?
- Half a million net profit for your firm in three years?
- 100 extra dollars a week to help pay the bills?

It doesn't matter where you are on the income scale. If for no other reason, inflation demands ever-increasing earnings. The businessman or businesswoman at the head of an industry needs profits to plow back in order to sustain growth. The worker needs extra cash to house and provide for his family. The person on limited financial means may simply want a job. In every case, money is essential. In most cases, it's hard to get.

How do you begin?

Work to Work

America was in the depths of economic depression when Mary C. Crowley, a young housewife and mother, decided she was going to find a job.

Her neighbor thought she was crazy when she put on her best dress and went downtown. But Mary had done her homework well: She looked tidy and professional;

she had developed a perfect smile; and she had practiced getting a job in ten different ways. When she arrived in town she headed for the most desirable store and asked to see the owner. A glum clerk directed her up the stairs.

Mr. Jalonick sighed as Mary entered his office. She smiled hard and introduced herself. "I looked around town and decided that your store was the nicest in town, so that's where I want to work."

Mr. Jalonick sighed again. "Young lady, have you heard there's a depression on? Take a look at the sales floor. The only time anyone comes to town anymore is on Saturday."

"Then let me work Saturday," Mary replied.

Mr. Jalonick looked doubtful, so she added, "And if I don't sell enough to more than pay my salary, you don't have to let me come back."

That got to him. Mary went home (the neighbor almost collapsed when she heard the news) and pondered how she could make the most of her opportunity. After much prayer and consideration she had an idea. Everything in the store was priced three cents off the dollars—$.97, $1.97, and so on. This meant that every customer had to wait for change. Wasn't it possible, Mary thought, to persuade a customer to spend three more cents and avoid waiting?

On Saturday morning she noticed a rack of spools by the central counter. The spools were four cents each. "For only a penny more," said Mary to her customers, "you can have your choice of spoon thread, and you won't have to wait for change." She would smile broadly. "I'm sure you could use some thread at home."

Nine out of ten customers could. Mary sold more that day than any other sales clerk.

"You certainly are a hard worker," said Mr. Jalonick at the end of the day.

Mary laughed. "You call this work? I call it fun. I've never enjoyed anything so much in my life."

That Saturday was the launch of an amazingly successful career in sales. Who would have thought that a young mother could land a job like this in the midst of the depression?

From a young married woman who faithfully attended church and sang in the choir Sunday by Sunday in a gingham dress to the lauded businesswoman whose company did more than half a billion dollars when she passed away in 1987, she demonstrated the TOP principles.

Mary *trusted* in God, she *organized* to succeed, and she *persisted* until she got what she wanted. She started as a TOP employee and ended up as a TOP employer.

Motive and Motivation

With the TOP principles of trust, organization, and persistence, you can expand your income. You can take your goal out of the realm of wishful thinking and make-believe and turn it into reality. You can transform your financial impossibilities into possibilities. But you should be aware of one point.

"There are," declared Samuel Johnson in 1775, "few ways in which a man can be more innocently employed than in making money."

If that were true, a chapter on expanding your income would be pretty straightforward. But "innocence" and "money-making" don't always go together, and this adds another dimension of impossibility.

For one thing, there's the question of motive. Every job, every business enterprise, is designed to achieve something. Part of that achievement is the creation of wealth, which in turn goes to feed and clothe and house the workers and to help the company grow. But the best kind of business vision includes more than finance. It concerns itself with objectives that may at first sight have little to do with the economic well-being of the wealth-creator. A good example is conservation. "Making money" can hardly be called "innocent," for example, if it involves slaughtering seals or wantonly spilling crude oil into the ocean.

Another kind of positive motivation in business has been demonstrated by Paul J. Meyer, founder of the Success Motivation Institute. Early in life, Paul Meyer learned from his mother the Bible verse "I can do all things through Christ who strengthens me (Philippians 4:13). She accepted the verse literally and taught her son to do the same.

The verse has become a kind of keynote of Paul Meyer's business practice. For his business to be done "through Christ," he must be convinced, through prayer, that he is doing what God wants him to do and is willing to use any success he enjoys as a means of serving God.

He began his professional life at 19 as a salesman. But he quickly discovered that the most enjoyable part of his work was the opportunity he had to challenge others to think about their goals, and to help them plan how to achieve those goals. In a few years he perfected for himself a way of helping people approach this challenge in a systematic, practical manner.

He then looked for the best way to turn this process into a marketable product, and chose the idea of condensing some outstanding books on potential-realization onto a small record which could be listened to repeatedly until the ideas were absorbed and implemented. So it was that Success Motivation Institute was born.

When Paul Meyer started his new business in a converted garage building in Waco, Texas, everyone who knew him laughed. They said the company would never get off the ground; they called it a house of cards. He started with a thousand dollars in capital and one employee, John Cook. Paul sold the records while John packed them in boxes, shipped them, and did the paperwork. Both of them swept water out of the office when it rained.

From those humble beginnings, SMI has expanded to over 25 different corporations, including real estate, aviation, consumer finance, auto racing, and charities. In addition, Meyer estimates that over the years "there has been an investment of over 15 million dollars in a total of over 40 other companies or major ideas that failed. Another way to say it is that 65 percent of everything I have ever started—either a company, marketing idea, or entrepreneurial effort—failed. Thirty-five percent worked."

One feature of SMI, though, stands out above all the others: *Paul Meyer is selling a product he believes in.* He would be selling it whether or not SMI proved a financial success, because his motive is not simply financial; he wants to help people. It just happens that helping people has made him a multimillionaire.

The Case for Integrity

To turn your financial impossibilities into possibilities you will need sound motives. You'll also need sound *means*. Let me explain.

In 1971 the 500 members of the Association of British Investigators met to hammer out an agreement on working methods. After some debate they rejected a number of techniques, including blackmail, bribery, phone-tapping, fake job interviews, trespassing, dummy negotiations, and the hiring of a worker in order to discover his former employer's manufacturing secrets.

Ironically, nearly all of these options are stock-in-trade for the modern television cop. But the fact that a group of real sleuths once got together to agree on a code of practice indicates that even private investigative work is not beyond the reach of morality. In business generally there has been a background awareness, not just of the need to behave well, but of the duty placed on the business community to set a good example.

Note this thundering rebuke from *Forbes* magazine in October 1917:

> If business cannot be conducted under the existing economic order clearly, honorably, ethically and humanely, then it ought to be swept away, and something different established in its stead.

A similar sentiment was expressed in 1961 by Henry Ford II:

> A corporation ... is a purposeful organization that can and must give more than just money to those who serve it, and those it serves. It should reflect in its daily actions the principles and aspirations of our society in its finest tradition.[1]

But good conscience isn't the only force acting on business behavior as we move into the 1990's. Much more acute is the pressure to keep options open just in case being Mr. Nice Guy doesn't pay. When your whole enterprise is on the line, morality can become a nuisance. And what responsible executive would not reserve a margin of "ethical flexibility" in the face of financial disaster?

As you move to expand your income you will be tempted to cut moral corners. After all, who's going to find out if you make private use of your expense account? What does it really matter if you lie on an application form or "borrow" some equipment from the office? Why go out of your way to give your employees good pay or your customers a fair price? And isn't shady dealing just a part of business life in the twentieth century?

The biblical answer to these questions is simple: Integrity pays. It doesn't matter what you're doing or how much you earn; there are two principles that are the TOP solution to income expansion:

1. That right and wrong business practices remain right and wrong under all circumstances.
2. That integrity in business, far from being a liability is in fact the key to success.

Integrity in Action

P.K.D. Lee worked for a while as head of the mechanical department of India's Southern Railway, Madras Division.

As a Christian, Lee had over the years developed a reputation for uncompromising honesty. This was not viewed as an asset in a government service which made a fine art of passing the buck and preferred "satisfactory" reports to true ones. In fact, it was probably by mistake that Lee was posted to Madras—a division with more problems to hide than most, thus highly sensitive.

Almost as soon as he arrived he noticed a suspicious regularity in the number of "unfit" railroad cars reported from the main yard—always 250. The figure remained constant over the next few months, though it was clear to Lee when he visited the yard that it was a gross underestimate. He demanded a census, and when this too showed 250 unfit railroad cars he summoned the employees responsible and threatened them with disciplinary action if they didn't report the true figure. The next day it came out—860. Shock waves reverberated through the department. A month later Lee was moved.

Had the story ended there, it might stand—to some people at least—as a solemn warning to anyone foolish enough to let morality loose at work. In fact, over the next eight months Lee's successor at Madras ran into such severe problems that the bosses had to bring Lee back. As a result, the whole process of railroad car repair was reviewed, and the real number of unfit railroad cars was reduced to 300.

Harry S. Truman is famous for the sign on his presidential desk saying, "The buck stops here." In fact, he had two signs. The other was a quotation from Mark Twain: "Always tell the truth. It will please some people and astonish the rest."

Three Ways to Wriggle Out

How, in practice, does personal integrity help you turn financial impossibilities into possibilities? John Adair in his excellent book *Management and Morality*, suggests three guidelines.

One, integrity means *not bending the rules*. It is tempting to redefine right and wrong in order to accommodate some dubious act which we would instantly condemn in someone else. But nominal integrity, had on our own terms, is no integrity at all. You cannot be under the law and over it at the same time. Since morality is constant, observance of it should be habitual.

Two, integrity means *not making exceptions*. Adair makes the thoughtful comment that integrity can turn gaping wounds into scars of experience, "provided that the central will to goodness is not broken or wasted away." The resilience of that central will may lure us into small betrayals of principle, reasoning that "just this once" will do no lasting harm. It is a dangerous presumption that too easily results in progressive hardening of the conscience.

Three, integrity means *not allowing life to become compartmentalized*. It is not good enough to have one morality for social life and another for business, one morality for use among friends and another for use abroad. If we live with divided values, warns Adair, "several selves may form on the various moralities like ice growing around trailing fishing lines in frozen seas."

In the end, integrity is not about *what we do* but about *who we are*. That is crucially important. Long-term success in business and employment depends, to a large extent, on winning the trust of others—a trust hard-won and quickly lost. Consequently, the secret of being successful and straight in moneymaking lies in cultivating actions that reflect and reinforce our inner integrity. For managers especially, the stakes are high. Adair quotes this summary of findings from a British Institute of Management report in *International Business*:

> When the confidence of employees in their management wanes, respect and esteem for them may never be regained. For it is possible to possess all the elements of effective management save one—credibility—and the lack of this one will doom an enterprise to failure. Some of the more obvious factors in opening up a credibility gap are disparity between words and deeds, the systematic use of words to conceal motives, uncertainty among men in authority, and the lack of contact between a leader and his employees.
>
> The four remedies are therefore quite clear. A manager should keep every commitment, act predictably, be consistent with his own philosophy in doing as he says he will, and lastly encourage the airing of dissent so that solutions are found.[2]

The Four-Way Test

This view enjoys a surprising degree of support, as you will see from the story of Herb Taylor.

In 1928 Taylor was Executive Vice-President of Jewell Tea Company. Jewell Tea had recently acquired Club Aluminum, a company with a good product but indifferent management. The banks were holding paper on Club Aluminum. Its only positive net worth was a significant amount of goodwill. The president of Jewell Tea asked Taylor to spend half his time at Club Aluminum to turn it around financially.

This was a volatile period in American history. Little legislation existed to restrict advertising, so it was common practice for companies to make exaggerated—if not outrightly false—claims about products. Fortunes rose and fell at breakneck speed. And soon after Taylor's arrival at Club Aluminum came the stock market crash.

In 1930, Jewell Tea having just expanded into the food-store business, the president requested that Taylor return full-time to his original position. But Taylor had developed a sense of loyalty to his adopted company and to the young men he had brought in to run it. He told the Jewell Tea president that the banks would likely call the paper on Club Aluminum and send it into liquidation, with the result that the new staff would lose their jobs. So he reported to the president and stayed put.

As the depression worsened, pressure on Club Aluminum increased. It was in 1931 that Taylor, after praying in his office for the future of the company, took a three-by-five card and wrote the first words that came into his mind. The words were these: *truth, fairness, goodwill*, and *beneficial effect on people*.

He then summoned several of the men he had brought in as executives—men of various religious backgrounds— and asked them if anything he had written on the card conflicted with their beliefs. No one spoke up, so Taylor put forward the proposal that these four principles should become the basis of a credo by which to operate the company. The credo was worded as follows:

THE FOUR-WAY TEST

Of the things we think, say, or do:
1. Is it TRUTH?
2. Is it FAIR to all concerned?

3. Will it build GOODWILL and BETTER FRIENDSHIPS?
4. Will it be BENEFICIAL to all concerned?

The Four-Way Test became the central pivot of company policy, one major result of which was that the company started to be honest in its advertising. And it worked: Club Aluminum prospered.

Years later, in 1951, the Rotary Club of Chicago, where Taylor was a member, asked him if they could use the test. Taylor signed over the copyrights to the Club. Since then the Four-Way Test has been associated with the Rotary. It has influenced businesses in Taylor's native America and across the world.

The TOP Earner

TRUST. You can expand your income because God is interested in your business affairs, just as He is interested in every other period of your life. As it says in Proverbs 3:5,6, "Trust in the Lord with all your heart, and do not rely on your own insight. In all your ways acknowledge him, and he will make straight your paths" (RSV). Trust in God in financial matters is thoroughly appropriate and essential.

On the human level also, trust is indispensable to good business. Effective cooperation and motivation depend on it; credibility is shattered without it. This means that anyone from the CEO down will improve his or her performance significantly by cultivating the exchange of trust between associates. But note that *trust* is not the same as *credulity*. Trust operates on an objective view of other people's strengths and intentions. But at the same time it builds relationships and promotes operational efficiency.

ORGANIZE. Begin by developing a clear *vision* for your work or enterprise, a vision that goes beyond self-seeking ends. Cecil B. Day, Sr., founder of Days Inns grasped the vision of using his business to generate funds for God's work worldwide. Within six years he expanded from one 60-room motel to over 300 totaling 40,000 rooms!

Predicate all your actions on the basis of personal integrity. Remember the twofold foundation of TOP success in business: 1) that right and wrong business practices remain right and wrong under all circumstances; and 2) that integrity in business, far from being a liability, is in fact the key to success. Integrity is not a technique; it is a personal characteristic which needs to be carefully guarded and clearly expressed. Integrity will get you into work. It will keep you there. It will pave your way to financial success.

PERSIST. Paul Meyer made this final point of his early *Million Dollar Personal Success Plan*:

> Develop a dogged determination to follow through on your plan, regardless of obstacles, criticism, or circumstances, or what other people say, think, or do.

I can't imagine sounder advice than that!

9

A WAY THROUGH FAILURE

Failure itself can be an instrument to convert impossibilities into possibilities. That is, provided you don't look on failure as final.

Failure is almost the worst experience imaginable. All kinds of feelings rush in on you. Your friends often add to the avalanche of pain:

"You've made a fool of yourself."

"Nobody's going to trust you again."

"You've finally proved you're not up to it."

"Look how much trouble you've caused for other people."

The galling thing is that you don't even have to fail in a big way to feel bad about it. Forgetting an appointment or spoiling a special meal can be just as devastating as losing a two-million-dollar deal or failing an exam. You can fail just by having bad breath or skin blemishes.

Worse than that, failure accumulates, so that before you know what happened it has turned from something you *do* into something you *are*. Eyes are rolled, sighs are let loose, and remarks are passed: "She's done it again. I suppose we should be used to it by now...." In situations like that, other people's tolerance is about as helpful as getting a can of hairspray for Christmas when you're bald. You feel thoroughly and irrevocably humiliated.

Does this strike a chord?

If so, welcome to a crowded and highly illustrious club—because the fact is, everyone fails. And *failure is okay*.

On December 23, 1988, the United Technologies Corporation published this short prose-poem in *The Wall Street Journal*:

> You've failed many times,
> although you don't remember.
> You fell down the first time
> you tried to walk.
> You almost drowned the first
> time you tried to swim.
> Did you hit the ball
> the first time you swung a bat?
> Heavy hitters, the ones who
> hit the most home runs,
> also strike out a lot.
> R.H. Macy failed seven times
> before his store in New York
> caught on.
> English novelist John Creasey got
> 733 rejection slips before he
> published 564 books.
> Babe Ruth struck out 1330 times but he also hit
> 714 home runs.
> Don't worry about failure.
> Worry about the chances you miss
> when you don't even try.

The point is that *success and failure come in the same package*. When we say that someone is successful, we don't mean he never makes mistakes; we mean that his successes outweigh his failures. Nobody is a complete success. By the same token, nobody is a complete failure. You can *feel* a complete failure of course. And that's the catch, because feelings not only dominate self-perception but affect performance. They reproduce the conditions that make failure more likely. By this mechanism, failure breeds failure, just as success, in the famous dictum, breeds success.

The first move in effecting the impossible comeback is one of *interception*. Control those feelings. Remember: Failure in itself is insignificant—*it's what you do afterward that counts*. Accept failure as a final, absolute, and incontrovertible judgment of your potential, and you will fail for the rest of your life. *Use* failure as a resource and an opportunity, and it can be the door to great success.

Where Do You Go from Bottom?

If other people view a particular experience in your life as a failure, but you view it differently, you have stronger inner resources to draw from while swimming against the current. But if you view failure as just failure, the long-term effects can be devastating.

Whether it's the six-year-old clinging tightly to a spelling paper dotted with bright red markings and stapled to a note from the teacher, or a mature adult watching as the contents of his business are auctioned off to the loud gavel of bankruptcy, the pain is the same—that lonely, sick feeling that comes uninvited when we know we have failed.

In your lifetime, you will experience both major and minor forms of failure. But to the child of God there is no more life-shaking failure than that which comes from the result of making a decision deliberately out of the will of God. I have a friend who did just that.

Allison, now near fifty, has spent all her life in writing, music, radio, and television. Most of those years she has worked for or with various Christian organizations in a creative capacity. She also had her own personal ministry, speaking and singing nationally to churches, conferences, and retreats of all kinds.

Her first marriage, which lasted a good many years, was a difficult one and eventually ended in divorce, leaving her a single parent with two teenage children, struggling to survive in the Christian world.

Emotionally wrung out, bitter, and angry, she fell too quickly into a new relationship—one she knew from the start could in no way be what God wanted for her life.

Allison was a child of God and had been in ministry all her life. Yet now she found herself allowing her personal needs to far outweigh the importance of God in a major decision of life.

> I felt it should be my turn. I had suffered. I had worked hard. Now I wanted to have the things I had always wanted, and so I married him.
>
> Even on that day, I remember standing there and knowing I was making a decision deliberately out of the will of God.

What followed that decision would fill another book, but God loves His children, and He does not allow them to make those kinds of decisions unnoticed. The years that followed were devastating ones, filled with the kinds of things you read in *McCall's* magazine—things that always happen to somebody else. Allison's marriage, which she felt would fill her personal need, left her a victim of abuse and alcoholism.

> "It was a horrible, horrible time," said Allison. "In the process I lost my job, my career, my income, and my ministry. And I spent a year on the welfare line for food stamps."

After she hit bottom, Allison couldn't believe that anyone could use failure as a resource and an opportunity. She knew *she* couldn't.

The failure came not just because of her wrong decision, but because she failed both as a person and as a parent (as she took her children through that experience with her). She can never forget the day her adopted son said to her, "Mom, you know, it's really tough to have three fathers and none of them wants me."

There were days when she couldn't pray. There were days when she felt God would punish her and she would never think again. She couldn't write. She couldn't create. She was sick. She was emotionally run-down. If she had not had children, she would never have put her foot on the floor.

The only thing she clung to was the Psalms and the words of David, those words of repentance in Psalm 51:1-3, the tears of "what do I do now, and where do I go from here?"

That was eight years ago. Today Allison is again in ministry. It didn't happen overnight, and it didn't happen without struggle. It resulted from two things: Number one, God is powerful enough to forgive; and number two, He is powerful in enabling us to begin to forgive ourselves.

The key to overcoming failure—devastating, life-shaking failure—is allowing God to help you forgive yourself. God chastises those He loves, but He also restores. Allison said:

> I've managed to fail in every area of my life. And I know God will not go back and reverse the decisions I've made. I will live with the ramifications of those decisions. But His grace and His love are helping me to accept this and learn from those mistakes.

By the grace of God, Allison now knows that one can use failure as a resource and an opportunity. It hasn't been easy for her, but she has turned her impossibility into a possibility and an actuality. Today her two older children are in a Christian university and doing well. She is doing freelance writing, producing a Christian drama each week, and preparing to write a book. Her son tells his young friends, "God knows better than you do where you're supposed to end up."

The Noble Art of Buck-Passing

The TOP approach to rectifying failure is general, and you can apply it in a great variety of situations. The fact is that you can fail as a mother, a son, an artist, an athlete, or even a conversationalist. In other words, it's possible to fail at anything.

This raises a question. Since there are an almost-infinite number of ways to fail, isn't it likely that the failures are too diverse to be turned around with a single program? Shouldn't we, for example, distinguish between failure caused by personal incompetence and failure caused by external circumstance (for example, flood, fire, pestilence, or economic recession)?

Let me tell you a personal story.

At a particularly low point in my stint as a student pastor, I received a visit from my father. I was almost to the point of resigning my position and quitting the ministry altogether. Dad's advice has stayed with me: "If you have done poorly in presenting your message, analyze why it was. If the reason lies in your failure to give sufficient preparation, or to undergird it with sufficient prayer, or through any other personal fault, confess it, claim God's forgiveness, and go forward ready to honor the Lord on your next opportunity. If, on the other hand, the problem is outside yourself, commit that also to the Lord. If anything can be done about it, do it. If not, relax and rejoice that He is more interested in His work than you are."

Dad saw clearly the difference between personal and circumstantial failure. Yet his advice was, *Look to your own heart first.* Don't presume you can blame the circumstances until you've exonerated yourself. To put it bluntly, whatever the nature of the failure, the starting point is always the same: *you.*

Note two vital points here.

First, be willing to assume accountability. It may be that your involvement was indirect—that you were, for example, the boss of the person who actually made the blunder. If so, the temptation will be to pass the buck and act as though it were entirely the other person's fault. Beware! As a leader you willingly take the credit for the group's successes, and accordingly you must share the blame for its mistakes. Not to do so will lead to the group's loss of morale and will threaten future performance.

Second, never delay. In 1969 I discovered that our accountant had forgotten my instructions to pay an airline bill of nearly 50,000 dollars for bringing participants and faculty to the first session of the Haggai Institute. It was a simple mistake—he had paid another set of bills instead. The result was that we had no money left over to pay the airline. At that point I should have confronted the issue and required correction. But I didn't because I didn't want to embarrass our account executive. I waited, hoping the shortfall could be covered. It wasn't. Consequently, by the time I faced the accountant about the mistake, we had lost our airline credit cards and were on the verge of being sued.

I prayed as though everything depended on God and worked with the airline as though everything depended on me. It took two and a half years, but, thank God, we finally resolved the problem to the satisfaction of the airline.

Snakes and Ladders

Turning around the impossibility of failure begins with self-analysis. Your first reaction, like anybody else's, will be to protest your innocence. This is why two good rules of thumb are as follows:

1. The failure occurred as a result of decisions for which you were responsible; and

2. The more you want to deny this fact, the more likely it is to be true.

Don't be too hasty to let yourself off the hook. If nothing else, genuinely homemade failures have the advantage of being more easily rectifiable than disasters resulting from earthquakes, hurricanes, and unpredictable movement in the Dow-Jones Index and consumer taste.

What are the elements in a good program?

If you want to turn impossibility into possibility after a failure, you'll need to implement a five-stage program:

1. Survey the damage—How bad is it?
2. Evaluate the error—Why did it happen?
3. Eliminate the causes—Digging out the roots.
4. Salvage what's left—Saving the wreck.
5. Revise your approach—Reinvent the wheel if necessary.

How Bad Is It?

I'm no stranger to the unpleasant task of damage assessment. When we first launched the Haggai Institute for Advanced Leadership Training, we took enormous care to pick the right location. The last thing we wanted was for Third World leaders to return to their countries under suspicion of being recruited by the American CIA. Therefore, building the center in America was out of the question. But which country qualified as neutral? Eventually two factors swayed us:

A host of leaders from Asia, Africa, Australia, and South America recommended that we choose Switzerland. And we were offered a bargain price for a nearly completed Swiss chalet. It looked like an ideal location.

To cut a long story short, the seller welshed on the deal. His own lawyer resigned in disgust. We lost 55,000 dollars in cash. We could have retrieved the money with a court action, since we had an open-and-shut case. But we didn't want to dishonor God or embarrass God's people.

What made matters worse was that one of our major donors had borrowed 100,000 dollars to get the sessions started. I would sooner have taken a flogging than tell him of the loss.

"Why don't you tell me by phone what's on your mind?" he asked.

I replied, "I'm afraid I must sit in front of you and look you in the eyes."

I did exactly that. When I had finished, and to my great surprise, his face broke into a broad grin. "John," he said, "you learned a great lesson by a much cheaper blunder than I did. In our business, we have just lost two million dollars on a bad venture overseas."

Naturally, it was tempting for me to save face by underestimating the cost. I didn't because I believed then, as I believe now, that honesty is the wisest and only honorable choice. Honesty has another advantage, too: It provides a realistic basis for taking whatever action is necessary to contain the damage.

Why Did It Happen?

It was when in Rome, "musing amidst the ruins of the Capitol," that historian Edward Gibbon decided to analyze one of the greatest failures in the world. The job took him 12 years and produced the classic *Decline and Fall of the Roman Empire*—six volumes long and rarely surpassed in its accuracy and detail. Unfortunately for the Romans, Gibbon arrived on the scene too late for them to benefit from his wisdom. Still, the book he wrote is an object lesson to anyone in the business of making a comeback: If you want to succeed, be thorough.

Few mistakes are as simple as they seem. Causes are often linked in a chain. You need to ask, "What conditions gave rise to the causes of the mistakes?" or even, "What lay behind the conditions that gave rise to the causes of the mistakes?" And if all of this seems alarmingly complex, let me assure you that the search of causes generally begins in one of only four areas. These are shown in Figure 9.1.

Haggai Institute's property problem in Switzerland must be classified as an *error of judgment*.

This is probably less common than *poor planning*, a typical example of which is the American who took a team of 30 people to evangelize an Asian country. There was nothing wrong with the goal, but he turned up in the middle of the monsoon season, had his operation grounded, and wasted over a hundred thousand dollars. The planning was poor because the leader never sought information on the local climate even though it was readily available.

There are also cases of *insufficient information*, where data are simply unavailable. In situations like these—for example, the ludicrous attempts at manned flight before the arrival of the Wright Brothers—projects have to be initiated on the basis of inspired guesswork. But even if you have good information, set sensible targets, and plan meticulously, your enterprise can still collapse through *defective implementation*.

The aeronautical industry has its own term for this: pilot error.

Digging Out the Roots

Losing the first property in Switzerland didn't stop us from conducting the first two training sessions there. It

Figure 9.1: Four Factors in Failure

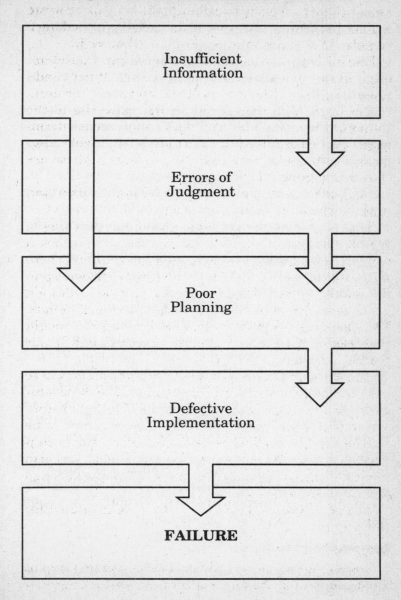

soon became apparent, however, that the country itself was unsuitable. Five defects in planning came to light.

First, at the time hijacking had reached epidemic proportions. We could not bring in participants from the East without subjecting them to a nerve-racking refueling stop at a Mideastern airfield where a Boeing 747 had been blown up.

Second, the Swiss climate and cuisine were unsuitable for visitors from the Third World. I noticed that, without rice, a participant from East Asia often felt hungry even on three square meals a day.

Third, although the leaders coming to Switzerland all spoke English, few spoke German. So if any difficulties arose with airline connections, they could not contact us. Most of them couldn't even ask for an English-speaking phone operator.

Fourth, the facility we were using lay 2½ hours from Zurich Airport. Just getting participants there and back was a logistical nightmare.

Fifth, Switzerland simply had the wrong image. To most prospective donors, Switzerland suggested numbered bank accounts, tax avoidance, and expensive ski holidays. To many people it looked extravagant to bring Third World leaders there for a training session.

It was considerations like these that prompted Haggai Institute's decision to move to Singapore. It wasn't an easy transition, but it did eliminate the causes of these multiple minor failures brought on by locating in Switzerland.

Singapore is racially mixed; its climate and cuisine are amenable to Third World tastes; it is 85 percent English-speaking and is independent, neutral, and within 3000 miles of half the world's population.

Saving the Wreck

What would you do with several hundred thousand flyswatters?

No, "swat flies" isn't the answer I'm looking for! Years ago a company manufactured more swatters than it could sell. The mistakes had come at the planning stage—flyswatters enjoyed a sizable market, but it was by no means as large as the sales team had supposed. So the company was saddled with the expense of storing a product for which there was insufficient demand.

One option at this stage would have been to cut losses and destroy the swatters. Instead, the company took the risk of engaging one of the world's leading persuaders. It cost them a fortune, but the gamble paid off. The expert, who spent considerable time examining the unfortunate swatters, came up with the line "These flyswatters are so square you can swat flies in the corners!" Within weeks the company sold every swatter.

In the business of salvage, this story represents something of a coup, though not every failure can be redeemed so triumphantly. Nevertheless, the principle of gathering what remains in the aftermath of failure must be grasped firmly if you are to make a successful comeback. I don't believe there is such a thing as complete, out-and-out disaster. You can ruin a relationship, destroy a business, flunk a test, or be fired. You can, like Job, lose everything that's dear to you. But you will never leave any failure behind without carrying with you the wisdom of *experience*. Take my word for it—that's worth having!

Reinvent the Wheel If Necessary

However bad the failure, you can still turn impossibilities to possibilities. But you will need to learn from mistakes.

Consider this somewhat oversimplified story of a comeback. A woman going to a speaking engagement in a remote country area gets into her car. Mistakenly believing the route to be well sign-posted (*insufficient information*), she deliberately leaves the map behind (*an error of judgment*). Not having consulted the map beforehand (*poor planning*), she soon takes a wrong turn (*defective implementation*). Being hopelessly lost, she realizes she will be late for the meeting if she does not do something (*she surveys the damage*). She admits it was a mistake to set out with no sure knowledge of the route (*she evaluates the error*), and determines to find out where she is (*thus eliminating the causes*), while she still has time (*salvaging what is left*). She pulls in at a small-town cafe. Here, it turns out, she has two ways of revising her *approach*—she can ask the waitress how to get to the meeting place, or she can buy a map.

Which would you do?

Clearly, since the waitress herself may be unsure of the route, asking her advice could turn out to be another error of judgment. The more reliable alternative is to buy a road map. That way the woman will not only get *there*, but also get *back*.

Here we are once more with Edward Gibbon and his lesson in thoroughness: *Effective revision of your system must go all the way down*—so far down, in fact, that it reveals not just your *efficiency* but your *integrity*. After all, the most penetrating question for any goals program (in personal life as well as in organization and finance) must concern ethics.

What is the story of the Tower of Babel about if not the ethical orientation of cooperative enterprise? "Come, let us build ourselves a city, and a tower whose top is in the heavens; let us make a name for ourselves, lest we be scattered" (Genesis 11:4).

William Goei of Singapore went through a chastening experience along these lines. In 1981, he owned a million square feet of office and shopping space, a beautiful family home, and a fleet of five Rolls Royces. But a local stock market collapse undermined his empire. His cash flow dried up.

In 1986 the bank called in a receiver because Bill Goei was unable to meet his capital repayments and interest. During the next year he fought a losing battle to free his assets. Finally, with a court hearing only two weeks away, he woke up at 3 A.M. and decided to pray. This wasn't unusual; he had been praying over the last 2½ years for some specific direction in his business affairs. But this time he was desperate. He asked the Holy Spirit to speak to him. He then opened his Bible.

The passage staring at him was this: "No one can serve two masters; for either he will hate the one and love the other, or he will be devoted to the one and despise the other. You cannot serve God and mammon" (Matthew 6:24, RSV). The scales fell from his eyes. His motive in going to court had been financial. Now, he determined (even though it went against his instincts as a business-man) to accept a settlement out of court.

The deeds were signed, and with mixed feelings of relief and restlessness at the settlement, William Goei planned a holiday with his wife. It was during the takeoff to South America that he read about the October crash on Wall Street. Suddenly he realized the wisdom of set-tling out of court. With the crash his net worth would have plummeted even lower, and he would have been financially ruined. He revised his *approach* just in time.

The TOP Renovator

TRUST. Failure doesn't have to be forever. But if you're going to stage the impossible comeback you will need to adopt what salesmen call a "winning attitude." Failure is only terminal if you allow it to be; otherwise it is a very useful form of education. In other words, trust yourself to get the combination right the next time around. As George Lorimer wrote, "While doubt stands still, confidence can erect a skyscraper." Bill Goei's confidence came from his trust in God's direction.

ORGANIZE. In terms of organization, turning impossibility to possibility in failure means maximizing your performance in six areas. *First*, and most important, you must acknowledge both the failure itself and the part you played in bringing it about. *Second*, make an objective survey of the damage it has caused. *Third*, evaluate thoroughly the errors responsible for failure. *Fourth*, eliminate the causes. *Fifth*, salvage whatever you can. *Sixth*, revise your approach to ensure that the same failure does not happen again.

PERSIST. "The course of true anything," said Samuel Butler, "never does run smooth." You will fail more than once. The more often you fail, the greater your chance to learn. The more you learn, the surer your chance of overcoming the impossible. Your success will be in direct proportion to your failures.

Allison is still persisting. Trusting in God and His forgiveness was much easier than trusting herself. All her life she had been taught that God forgives. But she had always had a self-image problem. She was always hard on herself, thinking she didn't do anything well. Slowly she is beginning to trust herself. She is a classic illustration of trust, organization, and persistence.

WOMANHOOD WITH RESPECT

Ever since she was a child, Joy Chatlos D'Arata has dreamed of flying. It was always her secret passion to soar with the eagles and tangle with the clouds.

Right from the start, though, turning this impossibility into a possibility was tough. Even her family and close friends didn't think she could do it. Some smiled knowing smiles while others made fun of her.

"A woman pilot? Women aren't safe on the roads, let alone in the air!"

Only Richard, her fiancé, took her ambition seriously. "Okay," he said, "if you're smart enough, I dare you to do it."

Joy ran to Linden Airport to take her first Cessna Discovery flight. She knew there was no turning back the moment the instructor let her take the controls.

Shortly after this, she and Richard married and moved to Florida. Her flying plans were delayed, and she wondered whether she could gather up the courage to start over again with a different instructor.

A week after she had settled in her new home, Joy prayed that the Lord would be with her and then timidly set out for Boca Raton Airport. To her surprise Joy was greeted by a woman. She introduced herself as Roberta.

"You give lessons?"

"I'm the FAA examiner here. I've been flying since I was 16." Joy must have looked surprised, because Roberta went on: "Yeah, I know there aren't many women pilots. In the 50's I was discouraged from working with the FAA myself. But women have made great strides in aviation since then."

Joy's first landing was a bit rough, but she made it. A few lessons later they came down, and Roberta climbed out of the plane.

"It's all yours, kid. Bring it around to land three times."

Joy's jaw nearly hit the floor of the cockpit. This was to be her first solo flight. She taxied to the end of Runway 4 and prayed, "Dear Lord, please don't let me mess up. Please don't let the engine fail, and please stay with me."

But her three landings went perfectly and, following the custom of most flight schools, she proudly hung a piece of cloth from her ripped T-shirt next to those of all the other soloed pilots.

From then on Joy's capabilities steadily increased. She went to ground school—the only woman in a class of 13. It was several weeks before she could get the men to talk flying with her. Still, her confidence increased, and she began to feel that if she put in her hours, she would always come down safely.

Then one evening she was preflighting her plane for her first night flight, watching another airplane take the runway.

"Who's that?"

Roberta threw a glance at the speeding plane. "Chuck," she said. "Boy, that guy knows how to fly." But then she looked again. With alarm she exclaimed, "That engine's not right!"

Two seconds later the sound cut out. In an eerie silence they watched the fully fueled airplane drift and fall. There was a burst of glass and metal as it hit the ground, followed quickly by a powerful explosion.

The image of that crash haunted Joy. For days afterward she couldn't close her eyes at night without seeing it again. Flying, she suddenly realized, could be a nightmare as well as a dream. Of late she had come to rely on skill—organization—to make her a successful pilot. But skill was no protection against fear. In the wake of the crash she was thrown back on her trust in God and on her will to persist and complete what she had started.

Persist she did. The day finally came when she climbed into the cockpit with her FAA examiner. It was a fabulous day. The test, though long, seemed almost effortless compared with her training. Driving back home with her signed-off log book, she felt a jubilation she had never known before. She had gained in confidence and tenacity. She had matured in faith. Most of all, though, she had gone for her childhood goal—and reached it.

Which Woman Are You?

One of the wonderful things about Joy is the way she has defied other people's expectations and done what was in her heart to do. She is constantly becoming what God has made her.

Sadly, as I look around America today, I don't see many women enjoying that freedom. Instead, they're under pressure to become what *other people* want. By "other people" here I don't mean just men. I mean the whole of society. We have a number of roles for women to play, and those roles together define our understanding of "womanhood."

Full-time *homemakers*, for example, often feel they have more to offer the world than their services as a babysitter and domestic servant. It's exactly the sentiment expressed by Gail Sheehy in *Passages*:

> If women had wives to keep house for them, to stay home with vomiting children, to get the car fixed, fight with the painters, run to the supermarket, reconcile the bank statements, listen to everyone's problems, cater the dinner parties, and nourish the spirit each night, just imagine the possibilities for expansion—the

number of books that would be written, companies started, professorships filled, political offices that would be held, by women.[1]

Professionals, on the other hand (who may be reacting against the homemaking role), often feel pressured to assume unfeminine characteristics in the drive to success against male colleagues. Not only that, but, ironically, professionals also feel the most pressure to flaunt their sexuality as *females* as a means of gaining preferential treatment.

All these roles are valid expressions of womanhood. Frustration arises either because a single role is allowed to predominate or because a woman feels she must occupy every role fully, thereby creating the most impossible role of all: *superwoman*. She cooks, she cleans, she brings up the kids, she supplements the family income with a full-time job—*and* she is expected to look ravishing from dawn to dusk.

Be the Person You Are

Roles are important; they're like sets of clothing: You wear different ones for different tasks. But your wardrobe isn't defined entirely by the jobs you perform. Even the clothes you wear for a certain job—like gardening—have been chosen to give a unique, personal stamp to your appearance. In the end you are more important than the roles you play, just as you are more important than your clothing.

It would be wonderful if the people around you—husband, family, friends, neighbors, colleagues—saw the essential inner *you* all the time instead of whichever role you happen to be playing when you're around them. But often they don't. In fact, they may expect certain things of you just because you're a *woman* and not a man.

To test how deeply this sex-stereotyping goes, answer this short questionnaire.

It lists 30 personality features. All you have to do is say whether you think a particular feature is more often characteristic of a man or of a woman:

A TEST OF SEXUAL STEREOTYPES

FEATURE	MAN	WOMAN	
1. Strong leader	( )	( )	( )
2. Good at showing affection	( )	( )	( )
3. Aggressive	( )	( )	( )
4. Ready to help	( )	( )	( )
5. Ambitious	( )	( )	( )
6. Childlike	( )	( )	( )
7. Tends to analyze	( )	( )	( )
8. Compassionate	( )	( )	( )
9. Assertive	( )	( )	( )
10. Soothes hurt feelings	( )	( )	( )
11. Likes competition	( )	( )	( )
12. Can be flattered	( )	( )	( )
13. Defends own beliefs	( )	( )	( )
14. Gentle	( )	( )	( )
15. Dominant	( )	( )	( )
16. Can be fooled easily	( )	( )	( )
17. Forceful in manner	( )	( )	( )
18. Loves children	( )	( )	( )
19. Independent	( )	( )	( )
20. Loyal	( )	( )	( )
21. Individualistic	( )	( )	( )
22. Sensitive to other people's needs	( )	( )	( )
23. Decisive	( )	( )	( )
24. Shy	( )	( )	( )
25. Self-reliant	( )	( )	( )
26. Soft-spoken	( )	( )	( )
27. Willing to take a stand	( )	( )	( )
28. Sympathetic	( )	( )	( )

29. Ready to take risks	( )	( )	( )
30. Yielding	( )	( )	( )
Total	( )	( )	( )

You may have guessed already that the uneven numbers represent so-called male features, and the even numbers so-called female ones.

Now go back down the questionnaire and check, in the third set of parentheses, those features that you would like to think belong to you. My guess is that you'll end up with a list strikingly different from the one under "WOMAN"—which shows how superficial sexual stereotypes are. Perhaps more men than women are "decisive" or "ready to take risks," but does this mean that those features are improper for a woman? Of course not! It's as ridiculous to say that a woman ought not to be decisive as it is to say a man shouldn't be soft-spoken or sympathetic.

The point is that you don't have to be bound by other people's expectations of you. You are more than just a homemaker, more than just a professional, more than just a female, and certainly more than the stereotyped woman on the questionnaire. Transforming impossibilities in your life has a lot to do with becoming what God has made you, and you alone, to be.

How might you go about becoming the real you?

The Homemaker Makes Good

Julia Stevens grew up on a farm in Illinois with no electricity or indoor plumbing. She knew all about hard work, but by the time she got married her education totaled five years in a one-room country school and six months in a business course in Elgin—not exactly a sound basis for a career.

A career, though, wasn't Julia's priority. She always felt that a woman should raise children, and it was only when money got scarce in 1921 that she thought seriously about earning money at all. By now she had a small baby daughter and was aware that if she wanted to work she would have to do it at home.

Her options were limited.

Then one day a friend came over. "Julia, would you make me some of those chocolates, so I can send some to my relatives? I'll pay you for them."

That was the inspiration that Julia needed. She made candy on her wood-burning stove and sold it to Miss Kingsley at the bakery in Wheaton. Miss Kingsley paid 90 cents a pound for the candy and sold it at a dollar. The arrangement was good, but not good enough. One day Julia asked her buyer for some advice. "I'm thinking of expanding," she said.

"Around here?"

"Further away."

"Well . . ." said Miss Kingsley, "why don't you try the Northwestern Station Shop in Chicago? I hear they're doing a good candy business."

The next Saturday Julia took a box of candy and went by train to Chicago. Mr. Fisher, manager of the Northwestern store, chewed the candy thoughtfully.

"I like it."

"Would you sell it?"

"That's not my decision. We're owned by Buck and Raynor Drug Stores."

"Can you direct me to their office?"

"It'll be closed on a Saturday."

"I'll try it anyway."

As it happened, the buyer for Buck and Raynor, Merle Hanson, had stayed over to discuss a new project with the president, Walter Krafft. Amazingly, they were looking for a line of homemade candy to promote in competition with three or four other candy chains. Enter Mrs. Julia Stevens.

It wasn't an easy deal. Hanson wanted her to come to Chicago. At that time Julia had just a thousand dollars in savings. She knew nothing about hiring labor or purchasing equipment, nor did she have any contacts in Chicago except Buck and Raynor. Still, she decided to move, and in 1922 she set up Mrs. Stevens' Candy Kitchen.

Everything went well until Buck and Raynor were taken over a few years later by the Liggett Drug Company. Since Liggett had its own candy plant, Julia was left high and dry. At this point—which incidentally came at the height of the depression—she could have let the company fold. She didn't. Instead, Julia developed a three-pound box of candy that retailed at one dollar. With candy selling at 60 or 70 cents a pound, the venture was a phenomenal success.

From then on Julia Stevens' business went from strength to strength. She married a second time, to Walter Krafft, in 1939, and opened her second major business in 1951— the Honey Bear Farm.

The list of Julia Krafft's credentials is staggering, and includes places on the boards of over 30 charitable organizations. She was the only woman on the Chicago Mayor's Committee of 100 Business Administrators for many years and an active member of the Chamber of Commerce, Executive Club, National Association of Manufacturers, Small Businessmen's Association, Laymen's National Committee, and many other organizations, both local and national. Through the Veterans of Foreign Wars she was invited to become an honorary life member of the Chicago Police Department. In 1961 Mayor Daley appointed her chairman of the Chicago Beautiful Committee, with Mrs. Daley as cochairman.

On her ninetieth birthday she threw a party for 140 guests.

Remember, You're a "Somebody"

Julia Stevens became a "professional" rather than a "homemaker" as a matter of necessity. Circumstances pushed her into it. Nevertheless, she made use of every gift she had, and in the course of her life she became more fully what God had made her. She turned the impossible into the possible.

Where she may differ from many women reading this book is in the comparative ease with which she has been able to function as a woman in a male-oriented society. She says herself that she never suffered discrimination as a woman. Yet I realize that discrimination is a major problem for some women, and it's not always their fault. Whatever role they play, some feel undervalued, unappreciated (or appreciated for the wrong reasons), or deserving of more respect than they get.

Often the blame for this is laid at the door of the church. I'm not going to try to defend the church's record on this issue. What I *will* say unequivocally is that the Bible affirms the woman as equal in every way to the man. But the roles are different as we learn in Ephesians 5. In Paul's words, "There is neither male nor female, for you are all one in Christ Jesus" (Galatians 3:28). The medieval theologian Peter Lombard summarized the matter neatly back in 1157:

> Eve was not taken from the feet of Adam to
> be his slave, nor from his head to be his lord,
> but from his side to be his partner.

But what if men don't want to be partners? I'm sure you can think of a few situations where a man is determined to treat you as sidekick, a piece of property, a sex-object—in fact, anything but an equal. Sex discrimination seems to be part of the package in some areas of modern society. Legislation is passed to remove it, but it lingers on in the minds of many people who have a say in your future. What can you do with an impossibility like that?

I realize that, being a man, I'm on dangerous ground here. So let me quote someone who has done as much as anyone, man or woman, to motivate the women of her generation toward success and fulfillment. She built a multi-million-dollar business from scratch, made her slogan "Think Mink" a byword for professionalism, and wrote a bestselling book titled *You Can Too.* Her name is Mary C. Crowley. I wrote about her in chapter 8.

Mary Crowley once conducted a poll among her employees at Home Interiors. She wrote afterward:

> When the answers came back, I was astonished. From all over the country the answers returned the same: "I just can't cope... I don't feel that I can accomplish anything... I don't have any self-confidence."
>
> So many of these American women, who had every possible freedom to fulfillment in life, said the same thing. They lacked self-confidence. They felt inferior as *persons*, as wives and mothers, as businesswomen.
>
> I almost couldn't believe it. These well-dressed American women were all "vogue on the outside and vague on the inside." They didn't want to be that way, but they didn't know what to do about it. They certainly were not Thinking Mink—at best they were settling for the "rabbit habit"![2]

Her solution was to encourage women to put God first in their lives. Why? Because, as she had once heard a preacher say, "God don't take time to make a nobody!" If God is molding you into a unique and special person, that person is worthy of respect. Do you believe that God takes an interest in who you are? Are you trying to become what He would have you be? Then don't make a career out of self-abasement. Learn to respect yourself so that others will respect you too. In short, "Be somebody!"

You Can Make It!

In 1980, Joaquina Pajaro of the Philippines received an invitation to Haggai Institute in Singapore. She wasn't interested.

Her husband, Eliseo, urged her to think again. "Why don't you go?" he asked. "It might be a fruitful experience for you."

"Eliseo, I do enough for the church already. I go every Sunday, I pay my tithes, I give extra when I'm asked to. Remember, I supported two deaconesses for four years while they studied."

"It's not the same as doing something yourself."

"I don't *have* to do something. I pay for others to do the work."

"*God* pays," Eliseo corrected her gently. "You just hand over the money."

"All right. But I tell you, I'm planning a trip elsewhere."

"Joaquina, you just visited your son in Los Angeles last year. Why don't you do something for the Lord this time?"

She went to Singapore for the specialized training.

Until then Joaquina's faith had been fairly nominal. Though she gave generously to the church, she clung firmly to the roles of mother and benefactor. At the H.I. seminar, however, she started to see this behavior in a new light. She was running away—from God, and from what she could become in God's power.

One day toward the end of the second week of the seminar, Joaquina's Egyptian roommate did not come back for lunch, and she was left alone. She knelt by her bed and cried to the Lord. She had been fighting a constant battle with her conscience, wanting to surrender herself completely to God, yet being afraid to step into the unknown and sacrifice the travel, shopping, and entertainment that filled her present timetable. The tension was giving her sleepless nights and anxiety pains in her heart.

"Lord," she prayed, "As of now I commit myself to serve You. I put You first. Only grant me three requests. Give me boldness to share my faith, wisdom to do what You want, and strength in performing my service to You."

Once she had made that commitment the pains left and she slept like a baby. On returning from the seminar, however, she was horrified to discover that God had taken her seriously: She had been elected in absentia to the post of Chairperson of the Commission on Evangelism in the Methodist Church.

"How am I going to do this?" she asked her husband. "I've never even been to a committee meeting before!"

But God moved aside impossibilities for Joaquina and transformed them into marvelous achievements. When she looked into the commission's work she saw all kinds of opportunities. She inaugurated a training course for church counselors, established evangelistic meetings, and opened a ministry for the women's correctional institution and a home for the elderly. Her whole life changed.

She wrote to me some time later and said: "I've been so busy planning and conducting meetings, I've forgotten about the leisurely style of living I held onto dearly for a long time. . . . I feel so confident now that whatever task is assigned to me, I can do it because, as Philippians 4:13 says, 'I can do all things through Christ who strengthens me.' "

The TOP Woman

TRUST. God does not see you, first and foremost, as a woman or a man, but as His child. You are the only version of yourself He has created. So be assured that whatever others say about you, you are loved and respected by God. He has given you a unique combination of gifts and opportunities into which you can grow by putting Him first in your life. Respect God's calling and respect yourself, and then you will win the respect of others.

ORGANIZE. All people, women and men alike, are given a unique calling. Some callings do not belong exclusively to either sex, though they may be more common in one than in the other. To other roles, such as motherhood and feminine sexuality, only women can be called. No particular calling, however, is forced on you *just because you happen to be a woman*. Nor should you allow yourself to be constrained by stereotypes of the particular calling that belongs to you. For example, God does not want you to be a "typical" homemaker; He wants you to be *you* in your calling as a mother and wife. You're more than your role, whatever other people expect. Aim to become what God wants you individually to be.

PERSIST. There's probably nothing more difficult in life than resisting systematic prejudice, whether at work or in the home. There are plenty of people around today who would agree (at least in secret) with the ancient Greek philosopher Aristotle that "females are imperfect males, accidentally reproduced by the father's inadequacy or by the malign influence of a moist south wind."[3] Are you going to let them get away with it?

You can turn the impossible into the possible if you persist. Win for womanhood the respect it deserves, starting with yourself.

11

A FLOURISHING CHURCH

If someone told you that a church begun with 27 penniless North Korean refugees would grow, in less than 30 years, to be the largest Presbyterian church in the world, what would you say? Probably all of us would say, "Impossible." But through trust, organization, and persistence, the little flock led by the young pastor Dr. Han Kyung Chik did just that. Today, the Young Nak Presbyterian Church of Seoul, Korea, has a membership of more than 65,000 and a budget larger than the budget of any church on the American continent.

Here are some of the highlights.

1. Dr. Han and the other refugees who fled from the North Korean Communists organized the church in 1946.
2. They had no church building, no printed materials, no money, no staff, no radio and television exposure, no church paper, no buses, no piano or organ, no hymn books—nothing in the material sense.
3. They were able to get a dilapidated tent under which to meet in the cold, Korean winter weather. But the water of the melting snow on the top panels of the tent shredded the tent, and they were back to square one.
4. They determined to build a church building. They sacrificed. One lady said, "I have no money; here's my wedding ring." Another lady said, "I have no money; here is my rice bowl and spoon. I can borrow my

neighbor's." Another member said, "I have no money, but I'll give my blanket. When my neighbor is awake he'll let me use his blanket; that's when I'll sleep."

5. Just as they were getting on their feet in 1950, having sacrificially put up a beautiful building, the North Korean Communists swooped down into South Korea, turned the Young Nak Presbyterian Church building into an ammunition depot, after the South Koreans had fled to the south coast.

6. When the refugees and their South Korean friends were finally able to return to Seoul in 1953, one of the men thinking the Communists had already departed, went to examine the church building. The Communists, lurking inside, killed him. His monument stands to the right of the front door of the church today. He was the first martyr of the church.

7. Dr. Han stressed evangelism, education, and social service. The church has produced more than 200 daughter churches. She has sent missionaries to all continents. She has established homes for orphans, for the aged, for the handicapped. She has organized schools. The list of spiritual accomplishments seems endless.

Be careful what you call impossible!
Oxford scholar David J. Lee wrote it; I quote it:

> You know the feeling.
> You get to the pulpit, or the podium, or maybe just the space by the piano at the front of the church. You're all wound up to give the fiery oration you spent half the week preparing, or the motivational address that's like nothing anyone's heard before, or the prayer that's so mighty it'll shake the roof down. Then you look at the congregation:

Six people.

Four of them elderly ladies.

Two almost stone-deaf.

Exactly the same people you spoke to the week before, and the week before that. In fact, all the weeks you've been here since you first came.

That "Will-somebody-tell-me-what-I'm-doing-here?" feeling affects everyone in a declining church, from the minister to the octogenarian who's been worshiping in the same building since he was a kid. The feeling crops up in other places, too. Churches hidebound by tradition (and believe me, evangelical churches can be just as hidebound as others) are often short on spiritual life despite their large congregations. Churches like that almost inevitably have pockets of discontented folk who feel—rightly—that their church has turned into a kind of religious social club and is no longer fulfilling its proper function.

For that reason I am not addressing this chapter only to church ministers—although it is the minister who has the most influence. Any member of a congregation, in leadership or otherwise, can play a part in developing the church's life, and so help smooth the seemingly impossible transition from death to dynamism.

O Lord, Make It the Way It Was!

There are two chief signs of dynamism in a church: *quality* and *quantity*.

It's important to give them equal weight, because Christians often emphasize one to the exclusion of the other. Those keen on quality will argue that it's no good preaching the gospel while the church is full of unsanctified saints. Those keen on quantity will argue that, regardless of the spiritual progress of converts already won, the church is obliged to keep pulling more in. (I tell you frankly that I would rather meet 500 nondiscipled Christians in heaven than to find only one discipled Christian there. I understand the judgment seat of Christ quite clearly. Obviously, I would prefer to see 500 *discipled* believers.) What both groups forget is that *evangelism and personal holiness are mutually reinforcing*. Will not the church with a heart for mission be challenged to deeper faith and commitment? Does not the church that lives by Christ's teaching obey the command to preach?

When I was a young man, the famed Boston minister Dr. J.C. Massee told me of a church that had voted unanimously to "call a moratorium on evangelism until they had developed a membership of strong saints." As he pointed out, this is a contradiction of terms. How can one justify an effort to develop strong saints and at the same time ignore the most persistent command of God in the Word of God to the people of God—namely, to carry on the work of our Savior to "seek and to save that which was lost"?

So, given that your twin aims are godly living and effective evangelism, where do you start?

The answer is: *prayer*. That's a rather conventional answer, I know, but I want to make a point about the *way* we pray. I'm sure that, like me, you've heard a good many fervent believers address God in terms like these:

> O Lord, we beseech Thee to send revival. Even as thou hast sent revival upon Thy faithful people of old, upon such as John Wesley and Charles Finney, so send down the anointing of the blessed Holy Spirit upon Thy servants, in order that we may proclaim unto this wicked generation the wonder of Thy judgments and the exceeding greatness of Thy power to save. . . .

Admittedly, that's a caricature. But it reflects two widespread fallacies about prayer.

One is that God feels most at ease conversing only in Elizabethan English and hasn't yet been supplied with any translation of the Bible postdating the King James. The second and far more serious fallacy is that prayer consists in asking God for encores—doing again what He has done before. Yet if there's one thing the Bible demonstrates with unremitting force, it's that God always comes back, so to speak, with a new act. He doesn't stand still, doesn't make repeat moves. He always surprises. What this means is that many people who scan the horizon for signs of another revival are going to miss the next "trick" that God has hidden up His sleeve.

Prevailing prayer involves *listening*. If you don't hear the promptings of the Holy Spirit while you pray, you'll end up praying for the wrong thing. So *listen while you pray*, and as God reveals His plan to you, make the accomplishment of that plan the subject of your prayer.

A man who prayed in exactly this way is Dr. Kriengsak Chareonwongsak, senior pastor of the Hope of Bangkok Church. He returned to Thailand from Australia, where he had earned his Ph.D. in economics in 1981. During the latter part of his stay in Australia, he received the vision of founding a church in each of Thailand's approximately 686 districts. As he explains, it was an impossible assignment:

> I set forth to start the church with my wife. I had no contacts, no coworkers, no meeting place, and was working full-time as a lecturer at a university in Bangkok. I paced much of Bangkok in search of a meeting place. Tears, sweat, toil, and much prayer went in to initiate the Hope of Bangkok Church....

Dr. Kriengsak and his wife had to look to the future because they knew so little of what God had done in the past. It was with great relief that they eventually found a place for the church to meet. The room, however, lay hidden on the ninth floor of a hospital. How on earth could they persuade anyone to come to such a remote hideaway? For several days they worried about this, and then they realized that if God had given them a vision and a place to meet, they could pray in confidence for a congregation:

> The third Saturday after starting the church, we prayed and asked God to send 25 people for our next worship service. On Sunday a count was made, and sure enough there were exactly 25 people. Encouraged and excited, during the fifth Saturday prayer meeting we prayed for 30 people. Lo and behold, 30 people came. Being full of faith, we started our all-night prayer meeting a few Fridays later and prayed for 52 people to attend that Sunday. Several counts were made halfway through the Sunday meeting, but they showed only 51 people. We got anxious waiting for the 52nd person, but just as I was about to start the sermon an older nurse came wandering in to join us!

The Bible says, "Faith without works is dead" (James 2:20). Not only did Dr. Kriengsak and his wife pray, but they worked. They had a plan.

He enlisted some key leaders. I know one, Mr. Maitri Modjaro, the owner of Sanyo in Thailand, an alumnus of Haggai Institute.

I can assure you that Dr. Kriengsak spelled out clearly to his people the objectives and the program of the church. He methodically and carefully laid out plans for staffing, funding, equipment and materials, visiting, and different activities to meet the needs of the people he was led by God to reach.

He demonstrated his faith by his works in an all-embracing goals program.

Goals for the Gospel

Today the Hope of Bangkok Church is acknowledged to be the fastest growing church in the history of Thailand. It has a total membership of 4700 and has had to move four times to house its congregation. But this aim of winning souls and making disciples wasn't achieved in a single stroke. Indeed, the church's present success is just another step along the way to fulfilling Dr. Kriengsak's original vision.

Your church can reach this same point of dynamism. But God will lead it in a way unique to the situation of the church and the gifts He has bestowed it. Study these factors carefully because together they will help define the opportunities open to you and the resources with which to turn potential into achievement.

Here are seven questions to get you thinking.

A SEVEN-POINT CHURCH ASSESSMENT

- Where is the church located relative to potential areas of ministry—schools, hospitals, shopping malls, workplaces?

- What pattern of social connection already exists among the congregation (present special ministries, kinds of people with whom church members are acquainted)?

- Are there time/money/location constraints on potential church members of which you should be aware in planning events and facilities for them?

- What social/economic needs exist in the nearby communities that the church might be able to meet?

- What physical and financial resources does the church have at its disposal right now?

- What is the pattern of gifts (in terms of income as well as skill) brought to the church by the core congregation?
- What potential is there in the present congregation and buildings for development and change?

Answering these questions fully and factually is a way of taking stock. There isn't much room here to suggest how this stock-taking might bubble up fresh ideas. Suffice it to say that a church in a neighborhood of young families could provide amenities and services aimed especially at mothers and children, or that a congregation in a busy downtown area could develop a productive midweek luncheon ministry for business people who normally don't attend church on Sunday. The secret lies in balancing the capability of the church against the needs of those who will, with persistent encouragement, come to Christ and join the congregation.

Bishop I. Wayan Mastra, for example, was sent as a young man to plant a church in North Bali. It wasn't a cheerful prospect. In the green, open terrain of his native South Bali the people had a proverb: *Nature smiles at you.* But in the north not even the inhabitants smiled. Christians weren't looked on kindly, and in the dry environment rice was so scarce that Wayan's wife, Ketut, had to take a nursing job to make ends meet.

Life was tough and dispiriting. But soon after they arrived, a young man came to tell Wayan about his stroke-paralyzed uncle. Realizing that he had been approached as a last resort, Wayan recognized the need and told the young man about Christ's healing power. As a result, the man became a Christian. They prayed together for the uncle, who subsequently recovered, accepted Christ, and joined his nephew in membership at Wayan's new church.

From that point the good news of Christ's healing spread naturally. The converts witnessed with joy and enthusiasm, just like those Christ touched during His earthly ministry. In five years Wayan and Ketut had five congregations operating in North Bali with as many people as they could handle. As the churches grew, Wayan recognized further needs: for food, for the exorcism of evil spirits, and for Christian education. His conclusion:

> You want your church to grow? If you are a pastor, be a true disciple yourself, keep spiritually nourished, and then feed your flock. If you are a member of the congregation, go and share the riches of Christ with those around you. If you are an evangelist, try to master the 3 E's: Be a good economist, a good exorcist, and a good educator.

Wayan Mastra's experience shows how naturally a church can grow when leaders take time to link existing needs with existing resources. It is, if you like, a process of making full use of the *possible*.

But why stop there?

One Flourishing Church

One of the most prayer-minded churches I know in America is Christ Church of Oak Brook, Illinois.

About 25 years ago God led Dr. Arthur DeKruyter out of a comfortable pastorate to plant a church in this small city with a population then of no more than 4000.

DeKruyter began with only five families. Today he preaches each Sunday to crowds about the size of the city when he planted the church.

While prayer was the foundation of that church from the very beginning, Dr. DeKruyter also had a specific goals program. He led the founding members to determine that they would offer the community service with no expectation of anything in return. They would never question the response of the people. To this day they do not ask anything from anybody for the church. They challenge the people to commit their lives to Christ, not to the membership of the church.

A second principle was to work on the assumption that people respond to opportunities. The lifestyle of the city is such that it is difficult to go into homes. People have maids, they are busy, and access is a problem.

DeKruyter, therefore, insisted on a program of excellence where everything began on time and ended on time.

He also made it clear where the church was going. He said, in effect, "We are going to serve you in six areas: youth, education, music, counseling, mission, and communications."

As he studied other churches around the nation, he found that many churches had two or three of these emphases. He decided that all six were necessary if they were to measure up to the opportunity God had given them in that community.

The church published its program and objectives to the community through newspapers, both in editorial copy and in advertising, and through mailings. They made it clear that—

1. The church had a vision.
2. The church wanted to serve.
3. The church adapted a program to the community lifestyle.
4. The church insisted on the same standard of excellence that Oak Brook residents required in their own businesses and social activities.

During the first five years they met in a gymnasium, amid basketball hoops and all the other athletic paraphernalia. But today they worship in one of America's most beautiful and commodious buildings.

The Executive Breakfast Club of Oak Brook, founded by Dr. DeKruyter, meets once a month and boasts an attendance as large as 1200. It is the largest breakfast club in the Chicago area.

The church sponsors seminars for women, for men, and for young people.

The church illustrates the twin emphases of faith and works. No wonder it flourishes!

Into "Impossible" Growth

Alfonso Briones of the Philippines attended a Haggai Institute training seminar in 1982.

The challenge to goal-setting and stewardship changed his life. Before the month was out, he locked himself in his room one night, knelt beside his bed, and made a commitment to the Lord.

"When I go back to the Philippines I will make my church the fastest growing church in East Metro Manila district, so help me God."

It wasn't long before he had second thoughts, however. Was he really capable of pulling off a feat like that? Hadn't he been a bit rash to commit himself without thinking of the consequences? He decided to hedge his bets. He worked quietly and prayed hard and consistently, pleading with God to help him. But he didn't tell anyone—not even his wife—in case he failed to attain his goal.

Early hints of change hit the congregation when he started preaching on missions and evangelism. The people responded well. Alfonso then shifted his theme to stewardship. The congregation responded well to this, too. Finally he started a training program with 41 young people from the church. Only on the last day of training did he pluck up the courage to reveal the goal that lay behind it.

"Let us win 200 souls for the Lord in two years' time," he said.

To his surprise, somebody stood up. It was Nelson Castorillo.

"That is too small," he said, "Make it 500 souls, Pastor!"

Alfonso was tongue-tied. "No!" he spluttered under his breath. "We can't make that. It's unrealistic!"

But Nelson stood up again and declared, "Nothing is impossible with God!"

"Do you believe that?" Alfonso addressed the question to everyone. At least some of them replied "Yes!"

From that day onward the church prayed for 500 souls. Through faith—and against his better judgment—Alfonso had ventured from the possible to the impossible, from what he *knew* his church *could* do to what he *believed* it *would* do. God rewarded his faith. Today Taytay United Methodist Church has over 1000 members. It has grown faster than any other church in the denomination, has spawned four daughter churches, and now supports seven full-time and two part-time lay missionaries.

Alfonso trusted God to take the church beyond the possible: He organized to expand growth, and he persisted with his programs until he reached his goal. His success is a powerful confirmation of the TOP principles as applied to church ministry.

Give Away What You Didn't Pay For

In the excellent book *I Believe in Church Growth*, Eddie Gibbs quotes this telling piece of graffiti found in a London office building:

We, the unwilling,
led by the unknowing,
are doing the impossible
for the ungrateful.
We have done so much
with so little
for so long,
we are now qualified
to do anything
with nothing.

This sums up the spirit of grudging cooperation with which ordinary church members are apt to regard their service for the kingdom of God. True, on judgment day they'll be commended as good and faithful servants and be welcomed into the joy of their Lord. But in the meantime do they ever get a word of thanks from the pastor? No way!

This isn't the stuff of dynamic Christian ministry, not by a long shot. In fact, it reverses the whole principle of dynamism because the attention of church members is focused on complaints and limitations. The house is divided against itself and cannot stand. By contrast, the flourishing church is one that has comprehended deeply what it means to *give*. Giving, after all, is the basis of mission. Christ gave up His life for mankind. Christian men and women give up their lives for God in a life of devoted service to the gospel. God, through His people, reveals His salvation to the secular world.

But this is where many sincere believers swallow hard. Doesn't the proclamation of salvation boil down in the end to evangelizing people, making them uncomfortable by preaching at them? As Rebecca Manley Pippert recalls in *Out of the Saltshaker*, "There was part of me that secretly felt evangelism was something you shouldn't do to your dog, let alone a friend."

This sense of embarrassment is understandable when you realize that much teaching about evangelism urges the Christian to close the deal early. It's a bit like asking someone to marry you on the first date. In crusade evangelism such directness is proper and fitting, but for the purpose of day-to-day witness by church members it can be counterproductive. Giving in evangelism means more than giving the gospel—it means giving time, love, practical support, friendship, pleasure, a smile. If nothing else, it's good psychology. Just ask yourself, What kind of person would *you* want to hear the gospel from?

The Target Grid

Finally, who *is* the person who's going to accept the gospel and join the church?

We have a lot of words for him: unbeliever, non-Christian, maybe even agnostic or secular humanist. All four words (and there are plenty of others) emphasize the conscious opposition of those outside the church to those inside. They also imply that a person's other qualities are automatically of less significance than his or her attitude to Christianity. For instance, your neighbor may be a pro-life campaigner, or a housewife and mother of three, but first and foremost an agnostic.

Such stereotypes, though, hide much information relevant to a Christian friend who wants to share the gospel. For one thing, a person who professes agnosticism may be either conversant with or wholly ignorant of the facts about Jesus. For another thing, he or she may be in one of a number of mental states, ranging from satisfied complacency to a deep sense of spiritual malaise. The Target Grid, Figure 11.1 suggests a slightly subtler way of understanding the people toward whom your evangelism is aimed. It's not meant to replace large stereotypes with more numerous small ones, and so it should not be

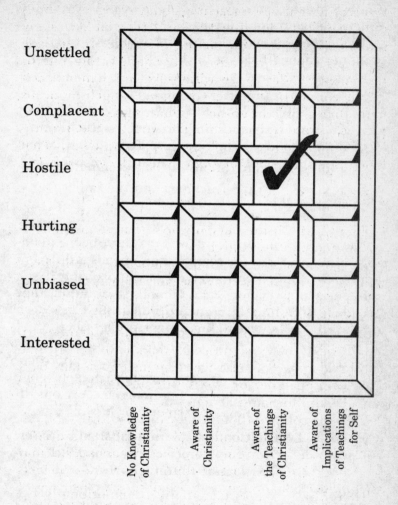

Figure 11.1: The Target Grid

applied mechanically. Regard it as a springboard for finding greater sensitivity to the needs of those who otherwise are simply "unsaved."

Along the bottom of the grid are four levels of understanding about Christian faith. A person who is not a Christian will either:

1. not know the gospel exists;

2. know it exists but not know what it teaches;

3. know what it teaches but fail to grasp the personal implications of that teaching; or

4. know both the teachings and the implications.

Clearly someone on level 4 (who may have been attending church services for several years) needs a different approach from someone on level 2 (who probably hasn't thought about religion since school). In addition, they are likely to fit into different attitude groups, as shown on the left of the grid. Thus a person might be:

UNSETTLED: Looking for fulfillment, or approaching or going through a major change in life, such as marriage, serious illness, retirement, or loss of work.

COMPLACENT: Comfortable and satisfied, with few or no perceived needs and little motivation to think about God.

HOSTILE: Intellectually or emotionally opposed to Christian faith, whether understood or not.

HURTING: Feeling the effect of a past tragedy, loss, or disappointment which now colors attitudes to faith.

UNBIASED: Balanced and open, ready to discuss faith as any other topic would be discussed.

INTERESTED: Positively seeking answers in the Christian faith and so already partially committed.

It could be that a particular person or even a particular set of people fit into more than one attitude group. The woman hurting from a broken marriage, for example, may still be unsettled as she attempts to find new stability in her life. Combining the two arms of the grid gives you some idea of the variety of unbelievers who live within a mile of your church. The square with a checkmark on Figure 11.1 represents the traditional secular humanist. Do your non-Christian friends belong in that square? Or do they fit somewhere else?

Young Churchmen Who Wouldn't Give Up

In 1950, at Bellevue Baptist Church in Memphis, a class of young men aged 25 through 29 got the names of young men in their age group who had no church affiliation.

The members, in groups of two, visited these prospects on Thursday nights.

They visited one young man every Thursday night for six months. Every week he promised to be there the following Sunday. He never showed up and, in fact moved his residence.

It took them several months to find his new address. Then they proceeded to visit him again every Thursday night. Each week for more than eight months he promised to attend church the following Sunday, but he never did.

He moved again, and they couldn't find his new address. Finally, with the help of the sheriff, they learned that he had moved into a limited-access apartment building and now had an unlisted phone number. A fellow church member, living in the same building, invited the visitors inside.

Once in, they headed straight for the prospect's door and rang the doorbell. When he opened the door, his face blanched. With quivering voice he mumbled, "I give up. I can't afford to move anymore. Believe me, I'll be there Sunday morning."

And he was. On that Sunday morning, when the minister, the late Dr. Robert G. Lee, gave the invitation for people to receive Jesus Christ as personal Savior, this young man went forward to make his public confession of faith in Christ.

Later he became a deacon and served the Lord in the church faithfully for many years.

To those who would criticize evangelistic persistence, this "prospect," now an active Christian, would say, "Well, I'm glad some people don't share your view, or I would still be without Christ."

These young men were TOP churchmen, weren't they? They *trusted* God, *organized* their work, and *persisted* toward their objective.

The TOP Church

TRUST. Without a doubt it is God's will that your church should grow both in *quality* (depth of commitment) and *quantity* (numbers on the church roll). *Trust* underlies the entire process of church expansion because conversion and sanctification are both works of the Holy Spirit. What you do to turn the impossible into the possible is merely a participation in God's preexisting plan. As Paul said of the church in Corinth, "I planted, Apollos watered, but God gave the growth" (1 Corinthians 3:6, RSV).

ORGANIZE. This does not mean, however, that developing a growth program is simply a matter of receiving divine instructions. Our participation is creative, and God blesses those who use to the utmost their skill and imagination in spreading the good news. This involves matching the *resources* of the church to the *needs* of the community in which it exists, thereby making full use of the possible. But that alone is insufficient. Neither the deliverance of the Israelites from Egypt nor the mission of the New Testament church were predicated on the use of merely human resources. Trust urges us to *aim* beyond our expectations so that we can *live* beyond them in the power of God.

PERSIST. Dr. Kriengsak of Bangkok and Dr. DeKruyter of Oak Brook, Illinois, persisted despite the obstacles and the extremely humble beginnings. Each, under God, turned an impossibility into a possibility and now into an undisputed reality. So if you want to see your church transformed into a flourishing church—as it can be—take a hint from these men and from Paul, Lydia, Moses, and practically every other person who has achieved something for God.

Stick with it!

12

EFFECTIVE EVANGELISM

(FOR CHRISTIANS ONLY)

Lori Cozart was a missionary at ten years of age.

It came naturally. For instance, across the street from the Doug Cozarts in Singapore, there lived a little girl by the name of Tracey. Tracey wasn't what parents call "a good influence." She used a lot of bad language, and Lori's mother Linda didn't like to see the two girls playing together.

One night at family devotions, though, Linda found herself sharing something she had read in a book by Corrie Ten Boom. It was about the Jews. Now it happened that Tracey's family was Jewish, and so the Cozarts started to pray for them more earnestly.

A few days later, when Tracey came over, Linda noticed her reading one of Lori's Christian comic books. She read it from cover to cover and the next day told Lori she would like to become a Christian. Lori promptly sat her down on the curb and prayed a simple little prayer, getting Tracey to repeat the words after her. The first Linda knew about it was when Lori came running into the house to find Tracey a Bible!

"Are you sure?" Linda asked.

"Of course I'm sure, Mother."

When Tracey came in, Linda questioned her to make certain she understood what she had done. She did. Not only that, but she added, "And now I'm going to tell my Mom."

Linda swallowed hard. "I think maybe you should wait a bit, Tracey."

But Tracey was adamant. So Linda committed it to the Lord in prayer, and a few minutes later the girls came running back to say Tracey's mom approved. Her only condition—that Tracey wouldn't go to church.

When Tracey came over the following morning to study the Bible, Lori didn't want any help from her mother. But she gave her a full report.

"Tracey has hardly said a bad thing all day, and she has started praying."

Who, me?

If children can do it, why is evangelism so impossible for grown-ups?

Probably because grown-ups fret too much about the consequences. "It wouldn't work," we say. "My friends would laugh at me if I shared my faith in Christ. Let the evangelists do the preaching. They can do it far better than I can, anyway."

But Jesus didn't send out a team of trained evangelists to tell the good news of His kingdom. He sent ordinary people like you and me. "As the Father has sent Me, I also send you" (John 20:21).

We find the idea of personal evangelism frightening. But the word "evangelism" has been emasculated of its true meaning. It's a great word. Unfortunately, it has been wounded in the house of its friends. The words *euangellion*, the noun, and *euangelizo*, the verb, appear 132 times in the Greek New Testament. In all but seven times, they are translated into the King James as "gospel" or "preach the gospel." No Christian I know gets upset about the gospel or preaching the gospel. If he believes in the Church and the Bible, he believes in the gospel. The word "gospel" could be translated "evangelism" just as well.

You may say, "Why me? I'm such a hopeless communicator." Well, you won't be the first person like that whom

God has chosen. Moses was always hiding behind his brother Aaron, but he led the Israelites out of Egypt. Mary was an unknown teenager, yet she became the mother of Jesus. What you are sets no limits on what God can do with you. Each one of us is in a unique position to witness to the gospel. There are people you know whom only you can reach. Maybe you are the only person they can trust. Maybe you are the only person they know who is a Christian. Maybe you are in contact with them at the only time of their lives when they are ready to listen to the message of salvation.

The secret of achieving the impossible in evangelism lies in letting your imagination loose. What opportunities has God given you to spread His Word? What creative ways can you find to bring the gospel to those God has set in your path? What special power and grace has He given you to transform missionary impossibilities into possibilities?

Only you can answer those questions. But before you do, let me tell you how some other people have answered them.

A Ticket to Evangelism

Professor Leslie G. Kemeny of Australia uses his work to discover exciting new openings for the gospel.

Leslie Kemeny's professional credentials are impressive. After graduating from the University of Sydney in 1955, he won a scholarship to become Senior Research Fellow at the U.K. Atomic Energy Establishment at Harwell, and he subsequently undertook postgraduate studies at the Universities of London, Manchester, and Cambridge. He is a regular contributor to TV and radio, has written over 200 learned society papers, and is the recipient of six international prizes in nuclear science and technology. At the present time he is a visiting professor to numerous Australian universities and an adviser to the Australian government on national and international aspects of nuclear policy.

Converted in 1950, Leslie Kemeny now worships with his wife and three sons at French's Forest Baptist Church in Australia. But his work has opened up a special mission field, for as a nuclear physicist he enjoys privileged access to the Eastern Bloc, the USSR, and China.

His usual technique when he's traveling abroad is to present his business card and an appropriate translation of the New Testament to the most senior official among his hosts. Later he will ask the same person the location of the nearest worshiping Christian fellowship. By doing this he avoids compromising indigenous Christians and puts the topic of his Christian faith on the conversational agenda.

His faith and commitment, he says, are frequently tested, but he has found that his weakness is a great opportunity for God's Holy Spirit to demonstrate the all-sufficient love and strength of Jesus Christ as Savior, Lord, and God.

A Wife Who Believed the Gospel

I believe the greatest obstacle to world missions, for Christians of every country, is lack of courage.

They look at the monolithic cultures of Communism and Islam and think, "It can't be done!" The early apostles must have thought the same thing as they contemplated evangelizing the Roman Empire and the distant, unknown lands that lay beyond it. Yet the command given to them rings in our ears also: "All authority has been given to Me in heaven and on earth. Go therefore and make disciples of all the nations, baptizing them in the name of the Father and of the Son and of the Holy Spirit" (Matthew 28:18,19).

World missions sometimes progresses in huge leaps

through the inspiration ministry of individual men and women. In *John R. Mott: World Citizen*, the evangelist's biographer makes this keen observation:

> His harnessing of decision to activity through a perpetual perfecting of skills and of strategy in order to reach an apparently impossible goal would be a sound guide for a young man steering his life into commerce, law, politics, science, engineering, art, or literature, as well as into the sphere of medicine, teaching, or religion. The significance of it seems to me to lie in the fact that he has dedicated and disciplined every power of body, mind, and spirit to incessant battle across the world, through decade after decade, for the Kingdom of God.[1]

If that sounds forbidding, let me remind you that evangelists of Mott's stature are few and far between. Most evangelism is accomplished through the steady accumulation of small, day-to-day acts of witness which, though demanding, are not beyond the power of ordinary people if they will only trust in God's help.

Kamala Rendy, for instance, a South African Indian woman, was reared in a strict Hindu family. She loved her mother and father dearly, and although she had known many Christians as a child, she knew that she had been dedicated to her own gods and could never become a Christian. Her marriage to her husband, Chin Rendy, was a traditionally elaborate Hindu ritual, three months after which she returned, according to custom, to receive instruction from her mother in obeisance to her personal gods.

It was during this period that her husband unexpectedly came to Christ. He had wandered into an evangelistic tent meeting, and although he didn't feel any different after he responded to the preacher's invitation, he knew he had taken a significant step and that Kamala would have to become a Christian too. He went to break the news to his mother-in-law.

She wasn't pleased. "You must make up your mind," she said. "Either you want Jesus or you want your wife. She has been dedicated to the gods and cannot become a Christian."

The young husband was confused, frightened, and frustrated. He had been orphaned at an early age. He and Kamala were deeply in love, yet if he were to follow Jesus he would have to lose her. He returned home in tears, and that night he cried desperately: "Whoever You are, God, I want You to prove Yourself. When I go to my wife tomorrow and ask her to come with me there must be no arguments; she must be willing to come."

The next day, he returned to find his mother-in-law and other senior relatives assembled to meet him. He told them his mind was made up and then turned to his wife.

"What have you decided?" he asked her.

For a moment Kamala stood silent, looking from Chin to her family. It was a terrible decision. She knew that to embrace Christianity was to sink to the lowest caste and to be banished from her family home. After a long pause she said, "I am going with my husband."

Her mother was heartbroken. From that moment onward Kamala and Chin were treated as outcastes, no longer Hindus yet still hardly understanding what it meant to receive Jesus Christ as their Lord and Savior. For many months Kamala's courageous step for the gospel looked like nothing more than self-destructive folly. Yet by making that stand with her husband she was advancing world missions, for over the next four years the life and love of Christ reflected in this couple brought salvation to her brothers, sisters, aunts, and uncles. Eventually even her mother came to the Lord.

Surprises in China

Aren't there some places in the world where evangelism is impossible?

As far as I'm concerned, the answer to that is a firm no. I first felt God's call to mission work in China when I was a boy of just ten years. Before I was old enough to offer myself for service, Mao's revolution had slammed the door shut on Western missionary activity, so I entered the pastorate instead. But miraculously, today China officially guarantees religious freedom, and I am privileged to see my boyhood vision realized in a way that exceeds my most optimistic hopes and expectations.

True, foreign missions are verboten. China permits the Chinese to work in the Christian area. Therefore, our contribution will be simply to screen applicants and provide specialized training in Christian leadership and communication skills so they will not only honor God, but will assist even more effectively in China's four modernizations. The work must be done by the Chinese—a method I consider to be the best, anyway. The most effective gospel work is done by nationals reaching nationals.

God is not limited by geographical or ideological boundaries. That lesson is brought home to me repeatedly as I meet the leaders who attend Haggai Institute's training sessions in Singapore. These are men and women from every quarter of the globe who come with their own special wisdom and then leave enriched by the sharing of new ideas and concepts in evangelism. Let me tell you two stories that have made a particular impression on me.

Dr. Mardoqueo Munoz is Guatemala's leading Presbyterian pastor. Although he was a gangster in his teens, and still bears the scars, Munoz came to Christ at 26, he was called to be associate pastor of the 400-member Central Presbyterian Church in Guatemala City. During this period he was invited to start a rural church among the Kekchi Indians, which he did with the help of a 65-year-old Kekchi-speaking friend named Julio. By 1974, when Munoz was elevated to the post of senior pastor, the Central Church and the five Kekchi churches had a combined membership of 2000.

Julio and Munoz started new ministries to help the Indian people. They launched an education program for the 99 percent who were illiterate. A health program was introduced. The Central Church bought three large farms and established an agrarian program in the Kekchi community. Everything was going well—until the guerrillas arrived.

Like many Latin American countries, Guatemala is plagued with intermittent clashes between guerrilla and government forces. As were many ordinary villagers, the Kekchis were caught in the middle. One day in 1978 Julio was approached by guerrilla leaders who said they wanted to help the Kekchis with education, health, and welfare, and that an alliance with their cause would benefit the local community.

Julio turned them away. "No. The Lord Jesus Christ is helping us through the church. We have health, education, and agriculture programs. And we don't have to fight to get help, like you do. Jesus does our 'fighting' for us."

The guerrillas then turned their attention on Munoz. By now Munoz was 33. He was president of the evangelical body of Guatemala and had launched a national literacy program through government channels. Nevertheless, he agreed to meet the guerrilla leaders, and for three solid hours he listened as they hammered home their philosophy. When they had finished he said, "I have listened to you for three hours; now let me have ten minutes."

During the talking, he had noticed that one of the men was wounded across the chest. Knowing from his own youthful experience what fighting was like, he started by asking, "Do you know that Jesus Christ was wounded for you?" In those ten minutes two of the guerrilla leaders surrendered their lives to Christ. Later in the same week Munoz also led the government's second minister of defense, a colonel, to faith in the Lord Jesus. Amazingly, the three were baptized together the following Sunday!

That's not to say that everything went smoothly from then on. In 1981 political tension increased again. Because of his nationwide influence, the guerrilla forces tried to gain Munoz's cooperation by force. Sixteen members of church families were killed. His own son was kidnapped. It was a painfully trying period for his wife and children, but he refused to compromise, and eventually his son was returned to him, safe and sound. On friends' advice, Munoz left the country for a while after that, but today he is back as national pastor of the Presbyterian church—a church with a membership that has quadrupled in Guatemala in just 13 years.

Islamic Confrontation

The second story comes from Ghana.

In his early twenties, a man whom we will call Salim wanted to be an Islamic scholar and teacher. However, he was converted to Christ on a visit to Accra just before he had planned to leave his own country, Burkimo Fasso, to study in Saudi Arabia. For two years he remained a closet believer, afraid to face the consequences of declaring his new faith in a devoutly Moslem society. During those two years, however, he realized from his close study of the Bible and the Koran that much Islamic criticism of Christianity was misdirected, and that God was sending him as a messenger to the Moslems. Sooner or later he would have to make a stand.

Salim entered Bible college, and then later came to a Haggai Institute session for training in evangelism. As a result his ministry took a dramatic turn. Salim had preached a series of public sermons refuting the accusations commonly made by Moslems against Christians. He showed, on the basis of the Koran itself, that "the Bible is true and must be accepted if mankind desires to see the salvation of God." It was not calculated to please the Islamic authorities, and the Moslem leaders quickly responded by challenging him to answer certain charges leveled against him, warning him that, if found guilty, he could be executed according to Islamic law.

But Salim was not intimidated. "I am prepared to be hooted at, stoned, or even killed if I am proved wrong," he said. "To this end, let the discussion be made public."

On November 10, 1984, in the Labadi Chief's Palace Court, Salim stood alone on the platform facing nine Islamic scholars before an estimated crowd of 5000. The men before him had attained a position that he himself had once coveted, and they were ready for battle. But he had no intention of debating. Instead, he dealt with every accusation by patiently outlining the teaching of the Koran and comparing it with the teaching of the Bible. For three hours he taught Bible truths to the Islamic scholars and witnessed to the thousands who had come to watch.

This was the first public confrontation between Islam and Christianity in Ghana. It infused the Christians with new courage and opened the way for Salim to train his fellow countrymen in effective methods of evangelism to Moslems.

The TOP Communicator

TRUST. Stories like that of Salim affirm that evangelism begins with *trust*. After all, evangelism isn't some harebrained scheme thought up by Christians to bully everybody else into their point of view. Evangelism is the reason why the church exists, a sovereign charge delivered to us by the hand of God. We engage in evangelism—whether to an entire country or to a single friend or neighbor—in the assurance that this is a work that God has called us to do. We undertake the task in humility, yet also in the confidence that Jesus Christ is with us, as He said in Matthew's gospel, "to the end of the age" (Matthew 28:20).

ORGANIZE. Evangelist John Mott is the supreme example of a man who organized to achieve in the field of evangelism. The evangelistic thrust needs to be organized; it was organized in Paul's time, and it should be organized now. But we must beware of simplistic solutions. I could have approached this chapter by laying down some kind of blueprint. I haven't, because you must develop your own blueprint based on your own experience and the demands of your particular situation. You may be a mature person comfortably situated in a small town in the Appalachians, or you may be in the front line of church work in the Third World. Either way, I hope that the stories I have told in this chapter will inspire you to think and act in a way that furthers your special contribution to evangelism.

PERSIST. Perhaps nothing is harder than having to tell another person what he is unwilling to believe. It takes courage, it takes determination, and it takes time. But reflect on the fact that God has called you to evangelism, and in His power you can turn impossibilities into highways of possibilities. How far are you along your highway?

13

High-Impact Giving

Once upon a time, in the township of Anyplace, lived a poor orphan called Johnny Goodcause.

Johnny Goodcause was a handsome, cheerful little boy. Nobody knew exactly where he came from, but all the citizens of Anyplace agreed that he should be housed and cared for. It happened that a special and very prestigious home for orphaned children had just opened in a neighboring township, but there was one problem: Who would pay for Johnny Goodcause to go there?

The citizens held a meeting. First to speak was Josiah Skinflint, a wealthy real estate broker.

"It's perfectly clear," he said, "that we have a moral duty to help this boy. However, it is also clear that nobody in this area can afford to send him to the Ideal Orphans' Home. Should we not pass him on to another township?"

Silence. Everyone knew that townships in this area were much the same, and if Johnny Goodcause didn't find help here he would hardly find it anywhere else. Miss Total Despair started to sob.

"It's hopeless," she said. "Absolutely hopeless. We can't even begin to help him."

At this point a cough was heard from Mr. Guiltpenny, whose wife was digging him in the ribs. He held up a dollar bill.

"Well, we're willing to do our share, the wife and I. Never let it be said that we didn't help a little boy in need."

"Us too," said Mrs. Peerpressure, waving another dollar bill.

Pretty soon the table in the middle of the room had 20 dollar bills on it. The citizens regarded it soberly. It wasn't nearly enough to even pay Johnny Goodcause's bus fare.

At this point Mr. Megagesture, whose sense of timing was acute, stepped forward with one thumb hooked into his coat pocket.

"I think the time has come," he declared, "for someone to take a lead. I therefore let it be known that I shall donate a sum large enough to keep Johnny Goodcause at the Ideal Orphans' Home for one whole month."

For this he received a generous round of applause. After this he sat down, with nearby citizens patting him on the shoulder. There was a general feeling in the meeting that the problem had been solved. At least there was until Miss Seedsower, the local schoolteacher, spoke up.

"And what's going to happen after that?" she asked.

The citizens frowned as she went on: "So far we've looked on our giving as so much money down the drain. We won't pay for Johnny Goodcause to go to the Orphans' Home because we think we'll never see him again. But hasn't it occurred to you that if we help him now, he might help us sometime in the future? Who knows, Mr. Skinflint—he may come back a rich man and buy some land!"

By the time Miss Seedsower had finished speaking, the table was loaded with money, most of it from Mr. Skinflint.

And so it was that little Johnny Goodcause went to the Ideal Orphans' Home, later entering the oil business and becoming the richest man in the state. Soon afterward he married, and bought a large house on the edge of Anyplace.

The Golden Rule of Giving

With which of the characters in the preceding parable do you identify?

Probably you identify with all of them. You know what it's like to give because you feel responsible or sorry for someone, or guilty for not helping him, or embarrassed that your friends will think you're stingy. All those feelings are natural. But none of them solved Johnny Goodcause's problem. In the end, even love—the fundamental human desire to help another person in need—*wasn't, on its own, enough to motivate high-impact giving*.

That is a significant point. We sometimes say (especially if we're Christians) that the chief motive for giving should be love. That is true. No greater motive can be found than the motive for which Jesus Christ gave Himself to sinful humanity on the cross. To feel in yourself such love for others is an excellent virtue. To express that love, whether you feel it or not, is a duty. As James says: "What does it profit ... if someone says he has faith but does not have works?" (James 2:14).

But having made that point, the Bible reverts to everyday pragmatism. In a perfect world, maybe people would give to the limit every time they saw a need. But ours is not a perfect world; it is corrupted by sin. Our sense of desire or obligation to give is countered—and often overwhelmed—by anxiety about the cost.

That's why Jesus showed no compunction whatever in appealing to the motive of self-interest: "Judge not, that you be not judged" (Matthew 7:1), and, "Do not lay up for yourselves treasures on earth, where moth and rust consume and where thieves break in and steal, but lay up for yourselves treasures in heaven" (Matthew 6:19,20). The assurance behind such teachings is that obedience brings a blessing. Give, and it will be given to you; invest, and you will see a return.

Many Christians are reluctant to apply this literally to money. Give in cash, they say, and you will be blessed in gratitude and peace of mind. No doubt you will. But I can tell you from experience that God is ready to return financial investments in kind and that He never gives short change. Note, though, that this is *not* a spiritually sanitized way of accumulating worldly wealth. Receiving money is merely a side effect of the fundamentally love-motivated commitment to give money away. If that commitment isn't central, the delicate bridge of joy between giving and receiving will collapse.

Give Courageously

Somebody who knows about commitment to giving is businessman Jesse Clements. Jesse spent the first 19 years of his working life in the Goodyear Textile Mill in Cedartown, Georgia. Wages weren't high, and making ends meet for his wife and two daughters wasn't easy.

His father, a supervisor in the same company, occasionally prompted him to move on. "Son, are you going to spend the rest of your life working in this mill?" he asked.

Jesse attended some business classes and began selling insurance. He soon found that he could make more money selling insurance part-time for a week than he earned full-time in a month at Goodyear. As a result, he decided to become a full-time salesman. Since his youth he had believed on the Lord Jesus Christ as his Savior and had faithfully tithed his wages. In 1980, however, in his new job, an entirely new vision of giving came to him. For 50 years there had been no Southern Baptist Church in a certain section of Cedartown. God gave Jesse the vision of sponsoring one.

Despite his higher income, Jesse knew he couldn't finance the venture on his own. So he began by borrowing 10,000 dollars for a down payment on 22 acres of land.

The move didn't impress his friends and family, but eventually God provided a mother church—Oak Grove

Baptist Church. Jesse sought God's guidance for the next step forward. After much heart searching he pledged to give 100,000 dollars to the project over the next four years. That was a phenomenal amount, especially considering his other commitments in tithes and offerings and in regular donations to Haggai Institute and foreign missions. Some people, in fact, told him outright that the idea of raising that much money was ridiculous.

Yet Jesse went ahead. Ten years later Worldview Baptist Church is on the map. It's a small church starting to evangelize in Cedartown and around the world. It upholds the teaching of God's Word and already contributes 30 percent to the denomination's Cooperative Program and other missionary causes.

Did the 100,000 dollars that Jesse poured into the church leave a dent in his finances? No way—God gave up front in just the same way Jesse did. Jesse told me recently:

> Since 1980 God has made possible for me to meet the 100,000-dollar commitment I made to build Worldview Baptist Church. He enabled us to secure a debt-free building, land, and equipment; blessed me spiritually and financially so I could support the Haggai Institute with 5 percent of my gross income and give 10 percent of my gross income to the Georgia Baptist Foundation; provided money for a scholarship to Berry College, for a supplemental salary to help Reverend Louis Pratt establish a Spanish ministry in Cedartown, and for the Polk-Haralson Christian Life Center. . . . God's Word explains it! "But this I say: He who sows sparingly will also reap sparingly, and he who sows bountifully will also reap bountifully. So let each one give as he purposes in his heart, not grudgingly or of necessity; for God loves a cheerful giver" (2 Corinthians 9:6,7).

Gifts Out of Nothing

Jesse made his commitment to fund a new church when his own finances were expanding. But you may want to ask the same question which Grace Sathyara asked me at a training session in 1977: "How can poor people, who earn only a moderate income, be expected to tithe?"

For Grace the issue was painfully relevant. For a long time her family had been poor—so poor that by the end of the month they were forced to take back money they had set aside at the beginning for a tithe. Now she was in debt. In fact, coming to the session had in itself been a huge sacrifice, since she had to take unpaid time off from the school where she was a teacher.

As I remember, I answered by telling the group about my own experiences as a child, when my father earned so little as a pastor that more than once only unexpected gifts kept body and soul together. Grace understood from me what I had understood from my father—the importance of giving God His due even when cash was short—and returned to Bangalore excited. Although the loss of wages incurred by her visit to Singapore had intensified her financial problem, she immediately paid her tithe to the church. She felt immensely satisfied.

Two weeks later she was called to the school office.

"Here's a packet for you," said the clerk.

"What is it?"

"Pay arrears for the last five years."

When Grace opened it, to her amazement she found almost the exact amount she had dropped into the collection bag at church! God had honored her faith. And He continues to honor it, for soon afterward she left the school and now has a job that pays her far more. But what touched me most about her recent letter to me was the care she took to prevent increased income from desensitizing her to the love of God!

Money makes life comfortable and even gives a sense of security. But I will testify that the people of wealth I most admire maintain a modest lifestyle governed by simplicity and the extension of love and hospitality to God's people. (Some, like the late Guy Rutland, Jr., even embraced a measure of austerity in their personal expenditures.) They believe God channels His money through them to fulfill His purposes.

The Five Commandments of Giving

If you want to start giving as Grace did—on the principles of trust, organization, and persistence—there are five points you ought to remember. I call them the Five Commandments:

THE FIVE COMMANDMENTS OF GIVING

1. Remember that God is the PROVIDER. When you seek to give, in a big way or a small way, the gift does not come from you. You have been entrusted with it by God. He gave it to you, and it is your responsibility to give it wisely.

2. Give to what you WANT. Your innermost desires—within the will of God as revealed in the Bible—are often the best guide to what God is seeking to do in your life. Jesse Clements wanted to see a new church in his hometown, and that vision gave him strength to trust in God's providence.

3. Give on the FRONT END. God generally waits for you to make the first move. He doesn't give back to you until you've given to Him. It's like the Old Testament story of the widow in Zarephath. When Elijah met her she had enough flour left for one more meal. After that she and her son were going to starve. Can you imagine what that felt like? But what happened?

Elijah turned up and said, "Make me a little cake of it first" (1 Kings 17:13)! But the widow believed God's word through Elijah, and the flour lasted for the rest of the famine. She gave on the front end.

4. Give with IMAGINATION. From where you are now, you won't necessarily see all the places God might be calling you to give in the future. So keep your eyes and your options open. One of Haggai Institute's first supporters named Charles W. Shepherd, raised 30,000 dollars for a fact-finding study preliminary to our training program. He testified, "I got behind the Haggai program because initially I saw it as strengthening the moral base of America. However, through that investment I got involved in the ministry itself, and though I had been a church member since I was 12 years old, I finally entered into faith, genuine faith, in Christ."

5. Give the glory to GOD. When giving produces results, the first thing you'll think is what a star you are—that you've worked hard, planned well, and sacrificed selflessly, and that you now deserve a large share of the credit. You don't. You're not a philanthropist because you have a sweet nature and live only for the benefit of others. You're an ordinary man or woman privileged to act as the dispenser of God's blessing. So if someone ever erects a statue of you in the city square, make sure some disclaimer like that gets written on the plaque!

Giving Through Business

"The institution that serves your need, not our greed"— that is the slogan of the Dwelling House Savings and Loan Association in Pittsburgh, Pennsylvania.

You'll find the Dwelling House office on the Hill in Pittsburgh—not a location favored by the city's bankers and financiers. The Dwelling House CEO, Robert La-velle, Sr., keeps it there because he specifically wants to serve the poorer people of the city. It's a real family business. Robert Lavelle's wife, Adah, supports him, and his son Robert, Jr., who joined Dwelling House in 1970, is now its secretary and chief of operations.

What's it all about?

Simple: Robert Lavelle is out to show that giving can be a matter not just of donations to charity or church, but of *business*. His company gives to the local community by offering low-interest loans, thus enabling local citizens on restricted incomes to buy property. Since he first started, home ownership on the Hill has risen from 10 percent to over 30 percent.

The company offers its clients low-cost finance, friendly counsel, and sound advice. Lavelle funds his low-interest loans by offering his investors the normal 5.5 percent interest instead of high-yield certificates. The number of savers with Dwelling House is rising steadily, and the company now has over seven million dollars in assets.

Robert Lavelle puts a lot of trust in both his borrowers and his savers. He has organized rigorously for over 30 years, sometimes in the teeth of bitter opposition from some of the city's real estate brokers. He constantly strives to make the existence of the poor known, and to meet the needs of the people. "That means," he says, "that you're swimming upstream and the current is rough."

There's a saying that fits Robert Lavelle well: "The only things we take with us are the things we give away."

The TOP Giver

TRUST. The TOP giver recognizes his own weakness. He knows he can never sustain his giving from the simple, high motive of love. Indeed, he does not regard himself as the giver at all, but only as the channel through which God gives. Trust therefore lies at the very heart of his giving, for he catches a vision of the work God wants to do and trusts God to supply the funds through him to see this vision realized.

ORGANIZE. To be a TOP giver, understand that giving is investment. God does not forget the generous; on the contrary, He blesses them in excess of their giving, and not just in spiritual terms. Apply the Five Commandments of Giving. First, remember that God is the provider; second, use your own desires as an indication of what you should be giving to; third, give at the front end and don't necessarily wait for funding before you commit yourself; fourth, use imagination; and fifth, give God the glory.

PERSIST. Giving is a long-term affair, almost by definition. A person who knows that fact well is Gus Becker. Gus graduated from high school in 1932, during the depression. At 19, a Christian for just one year, making $7.50 a week as a Western Union messenger when most of his friends were in college or career employment. One cold Sunday night he was delivering telegrams around 10 P.M., riding his bicycle toward town against the freezing rain and the north wind. His hands were frozen to the handlebars. It was at this low point of discouragement that he made a covenant with God. Right then he was giving just 75 cents a week as a tithe. He didn't know what lay ahead of him, but he determined that whatever God had for him in commercial or material success, he would try to match it in his giving.

Fifty years of perseverance later, Gus Becker has seen his tithe go up from 76 cents a week to annual figures in excess of 25,000 dollars. He has risen from the humble position of Western Union messenger to President of the Chamber of Commerce. "My material blessing was to own a business that let me retire and enjoy security beyond the age of 70," he says. "My spiritual pay is when a 53-year-old Christian says, 'I remember, when I was 12, you said something that has influenced my life ever since.' "

14

"IMPOSSIBLE"
HEALTH

I was not expected to live to be 40. As a baby I had cholera. At six, though I had been vaccinated, I came down with smallpox. Severe glandular disorders threatened my health during my childhood. A brutalizing auto accident threatened my life at 16. The surgeon said, "There's no medical explanation for this lad's survival. But he'll die before he's 40. We've given him so much sulfanilamide (that was before the days of penicillin) leukemia will probably take him."

Both National Life and Accident and Prudential Insurance Companies charged me a twenty-five percent penalty on my insurance premiums until I was 38; they were sure I wouldn't live long.

I'm 65. The famed Dr. Kenneth L. Cooper of Cooper Clinic said a few weeks ago, "According to the results of your physical examination, you should be functioning well into your 90s."

I'm very careful what I call impossible.

Seven observations:

1. I believe God miraculously healed me after the auto accident.

2. The doctors lauded my mother for the splendid nutritional care she gave me as a child.

3. I'm blessed with good genes. My father just died, a few months short of his 92nd birthday. He played tennis until he was 85.

4. I exercise vigorously, aerobically, and consistently.
5. I usually work under pressure without working under stress.
6. I perceive myself as physically and emotionally well.
7. I commit my health to the Lord.

What I say in this chapter is what I've learned after years of consultations with physicians, nutritionists, wellness experts, athletes, and sports psychologists.

I'm not an expert. But I rely on the counsel of the experts. I advise you to do the same. Every expert I have talked to agrees with some of the basics, such as:

1. If you haven't exercised in years, don't start until you've had a thorough physical examination and secured specific directions from your doctor.
2. Don't self-prescribe vitamins, minerals, and food supplements. Ask your doctor, but make sure he knows nutrition.
3. Don't change the course of your life on the basis of one book. That is, unless that book has the endorsement of a variety of acknowledged experts on the subject. If you read *Type A Behavior and Your Heart* by Meyer Friedman and Ray H. Rosenman, also read *The C Zone* by Robert and Marilyn Harris Kriegel. Don't go off half-cocked on stress control. Take the time and spend the money to know how to handle your stress.

THE TYPE A PERFORMER always moves, walks, and eats rapidly; is impatient with the rate most events take place; frequently strives to do two or more things simultaneously; feels guilty relaxing; is committed to evaluating his activities and the activities of others in terms of "numbers"; and believes that whatever success he has enjoyed has been due, in part, to his ability to work faster than his fellowman.

THE TYPE C PERFORMER combines confidence in himself, commitment to the task, and control over those elements he can control to overcome seemingly insurmountable obstacles and transcend his level of skill.

4. Don't become an oat-bran junkie just because it's the latest fad for combating cholesterol. I suggest you read *Controlling Cholesterol* by Dr. Kenneth L. Cooper whose book has been given top billing by the medical and wellness professions.

5. Don't conclude that because your progenitors died at a young age, you must die while you're young. My friend, Carl D. Newton, Jr., of San Antonio, Texas, was born into a family most of whom died before 50. His prospects for longevity were not encouraging. He has had several severe problems with a carotid artery and other vascular problems. Nevertheless, he is now 70, and he lives a full, productive life.

Now, be careful what you call impossible. Even in the area of your health. If you're convinced good health for you is impossible, you're driving a nail into your own coffin.

Sick for Fifty-five Years

For more than half a century, my mother suffered from pernicious anemia. At the time of her death, at age 80, she was plagued by nine physical ailments, any of which was sufficient to have terminated her life years before.

Some of her other ailments were emphysema, hydrochloric acid deficiency, angina, colitis, and cystitis.

Forty-three years earlier doctors said she wouldn't live long. One night, in 1936, Dad came to our bedroom and

218 / Be Careful What You Call Impossible

asked my brother Ted and me to be as quiet as possible because Mother was critically sick and possibly would not live more than a few days. If, at that moment, you had told her doctor she would live 43 more years, he would have said, "Impossible."

More than once I heard friends remark that Mother never complained. She was too busy cooking for, visiting, and writing people who were not as sick as she.

I can see her now making out her "To Do" lists, updating her prayer lists, scheduling her time, and recording events in her diary.

Up until months before she died, she wrote cards and letters by the scores, every week, to encourage people in all parts of the globe.

Her mild manner, soft voice, and ready laughter attracted people to her and obscured from the average person her iron will. She just would not give up. I think her emotional health came from her total immersion in the needs of others.

Three years before her death, one of her doctors told me that "clinically she shouldn't be able to walk, but her quiet will keeps her going."

On June 8, 1979, my mother and father would have celebrated their 56th wedding anniversary. While she lay in bed in a nursing home, about a week before her homegoing, Dad said in a semi-jocular way, "You're not going to leave me before our wedding anniversary, are you, Mildred?"

She didn't. She died on June 8!

True, Mother believed God supernaturally had blessed her with long life. But she hadn't presumed upon His goodness. For one thing, she demonstrated a disciplined nutritional control for which her doctors applauded her.

Her life personified the formula: Trust, Organize, Persist.

Getting Serious

Jack Foster was born in Liverpool, England. He wasn't a great prospect as an athlete. Both of his parents had suffered from tuberculosis, and although he did a lot of bicycling in his childhood, he settled down at age 14 to a dreary life of factory work.

At 32 he was 14 pounds overweight and in physically poor condition. By then he had married and emigrated to New Zealand.

On a picnic outing with his family he first thought of getting into shape. It was the weather that inspired him. He told his wife he would go for a run and a swim and be back for lunch.

What seemed to him like an age later he stumbled back to the car.

"What's wrong? Have you forgotten something?" his wife asked.

Foster didn't understand.

"You've been gone only seven minutes," she said.

That was impossible! He was sure he had run at least six or seven miles. He was dripping with perspiration and practically exhausted.

That worried him. He knew he wasn't in the best of shape, but he never suspected things were as bad as this. If he were like this at 32, what would he be like at 40 or 50?

He decided to get serious and begin a regular program of running. His search for a better body turned into an incredible and unexpected success story. Within one year of the picnic outing, he ran his first marathon in the amazing time of 2:27:50. At age 41 he took the silver medal in the Commonwealth Games Marathon at Christchurch, New Zealand. At 46 he finished sixth in the New York Marathon, in stifling 80-degree heat, with a world-class time of 2:17:29. It's a stunning example of persistence.[1]

Four-Dimensional Health

Maybe, like Jack Foster, you're not too thrilled with your state of health. If so, how can you overcome the constraints—lack of time, advanced age, other priorities—that keep a better body in the realm of the impossible?

Much depends on the body itself. The fact that you are a male or a female alone determines some of your body's main structural characteristics. Other characteristics are peculiar to you as an individual and reflect your gene pattern, your age, and your previous states of health. The last two are particularly important.

The body is in a constant state of change. For the first 25 years or so it is growing and developing; from then on it is gradually deteriorating. During adulthood overall health tends to decline with age, and this trend may be accentuated if the body has been damaged at some point by accident or illness. Consequently "health" is a relative concept. The health you can achieve as a 20-year-old is greater than the health you can achieve as an octogenarian with a weak heart.

But this does not mean that good health is beyond your control. You can't make yourself any younger, nor can you ensure, beyond taking sensible precautions, that you won't contract cancer or multiple sclerosis. But you do have extensive influence over the four major influences on your long- and short-term health: *nutrition, exercise, stress*, and *spirituality*.

Halve Your Weight on 50,000 Calories a Day?

Nutrition is crucial not only to weight loss, but in other ways as well. To maintain its functions, the body needs to take in regularly a correct quantity and balance of six food types:

1. Proteins
2. Carbohydrates

3. Fats
4. Vitamins
5. Minerals
6. Water

How effectively these are introduced into the body depends on the total pattern of your diet. Depending on your age, activity, and body structure, you will require greater or lesser amounts of each food—though 50,000 calories may be just a little over the top! Still, there are a few basic guidelines you'll do well to follow:

THE ABCD OF GOOD EATING

A. If you can, use foods in their natural state. Refining tends to wipe out vitamins and minerals; white flour, for example, has only 25 percent of the Vitamin B_6 in whole wheat flour and virtually no Vitamin E. For the same reason, avoid cooking fruit and vegetables. Go for fresh salads. If you have to cook something, use a microwave oven or a steamer, since these allow more of the nutrients to be retained.

B. Cut down on foods that contain sugar. Sucrose, glucose, and honey are all metabolized rapidly. That's okay if you're just about to run a 10,000-meter race, but if you're sitting on a sofa, these fast-acting sugars put a strain on your body. You get all the carbohydrates you need in the form of starches from grains and vegetables. If you want to sweeten a dessert, use fructose (fruit sugar)—it's slow-acting, and it's sweeter than ordinary sugar.

C. Beware of red meats. They contain large quantities of supersaturated fats that will damage your cardiovascular system. Polyunsaturated margarines are better than butter; fish and chicken are better than beef or lamb. You can get high-protein yields by combining beans and grains, so don't be afraid to go vegetarian.

Vegetables, beans, and fruit supply the intestinal tract with vital fiber.

D. Be aware of the smaller substances. On the positive side, if you're not sure you're getting enough vitamins and minerals, you can always take a supplement in tablet form. On the negative side, watch out for additives in prepared food: preservatives, colorings, and flavors. They're not there to enrich your diet, and research suggests that some can be harmful when taken in large quantities.

Health Through Sweat

Reputedly, Henry Ford once said, "Exercise is bunk. If you're healthy you don't need it. If you're sick you shouldn't take it!"

Appealing as this maxim may be, it's totally wrong. Everybody needs exercise—young and old, healthy and sick—because exercise keeps the muscles toned up and increased the efficiency of the heart and circulation. Your only danger is if you undertake exercise that's beyond your capability. This forces the heart to work harder, rockets your pulse-rate, and—if you're mature in years—increases your chances of a cardiac arrest.

The trick is to set up an exercise program which starts out easy but over a period of about three months (the time an average person needs to get fit) gradually becomes more demanding.

Which activity you use is up to you. The President's Council on Physical Fitness and Sports recently asked medical experts to rank 14 popular sports for their beneficial effects on muscular strength and endurance, flexibility, balance, weight control, muscle definition, digestion, and sleep. Working on the assumption that a person exercises at least four times a week and for not less than 30 minutes at each session, the experts listed them as follows:

1. Jogging
2. Bicycling
3. Swimming
4. Skating
5. Squash
6. Cross-country skiing
7. Alpine skiing
8. Basketball
9. Tennis
10. Calisthenics
11. Walking
12. Golf
13. Softball
14. Ten-pin bowling

The minimum input time of 30 minutes four times a week is widely recommended. Listen to your body; it will tell you if you're pushing too hard. At the end of a session you should feel pleasantly tired but not exhausted. Your pulse-rate should be up from its normal 60 to 80 beats per minute, but not up too far. There's a simple formula for working out an acceptable pulse-rate during exercise:

NOT HIGHER THAN
200 MINUS YOUR AGE

NOT LOWER THAN
160 MINUS YOUR AGE

If you're 45, your upper limit is 155, so if you hit 160 take a rest. If you find you're below your lower limit of 115, work harder.

Stress Reduction

The Bible has much to say about stress. One passage

that sticks in my mind is in Exodus 18, shortly after the Israelites had crossed the Red Sea. By this time Moses, who started out as a political leader and part-time diplomat, had taken on the additional roles of judge, administrator, and social worker. Understandably, when he met his father-in-law, Jethro, some explanations were called for.

Moses made a feeble attempt to justify himself: "The people come to me to inquire of God. When they have a difficulty, they come to me, and I judge between one and another; and I make known the statutes of God and His laws" (Exodus 18:15,16).

But Jethro had been around a bit himself, and the story didn't wash.

"The thing that you do is not good. Both you and these people who are with you will surely wear yourselves out. For this thing is too much for you; you are not able to perform it by yourself" (Exodus 18:17,18).

The passage makes some interesting observations about stress.

First, it does not suggest that stress can be avoided. Being a leader was a heavy responsibility for Moses. And that confirms our present experience: A certain amount of physical and mental stress goes hand in hand with the drive to achieve goals. *Second*, however, it is clearly implied that Moses lived under greater stress than he needed to. He didn't have to wear himself out by presiding over every dispute. And *third*, he was not willing to trust anyone but himself with the interpretation of God's statutes and decisions. He had fallen into the classic Catch-22 situation: In order to feel at ease, he had to keep everything under his personal control, but the strain of doing so prevented him from feeling at ease.

Jethro's solution exemplifies powerfully the principles of Trust, Organization, and Persistence. Moses had to learn trust; God could minister to the needs of the Israelites without keeping Moses on duty 25 hours a day.

Let Moses himself worry about the big disputes, but the smaller ones could be dealt with by other people. Organize a hierarchy of leadership, advised Jethro, and so spread the load. That way, with a permanent leadership structure, "you will be able to endure, and all this people will also go to their place in peace" (Exodus 18:23).

The Holmes-Rahe Analysis[2]

One way of evaluating the amount of stress in your life is to tally your Life Change Units (LCU's).

This method views change as the key to identifying stress, and assigns a value to each class of life change. It is based on the research finding that deleterious effects depend not only on whether an event is positive or negative, but also on the adaptation it demands from the individual affected. In other words, even positive changes such as marriage and promotion can still be quite stressful.

To use the chart, simply total the LCU's for any life changes that you've gone through during the last year (counting double those you've gone through twice).

CHANGES	LCU's	SCORE
Death of husband or wife	100	_____
Divorce	73	_____
Marital separation	65	_____
Jail term	63	_____
Death of a close family member	63	_____
Personal injury or loss	53	_____
Marriage	50	_____
Loss of your job	47	_____
Marital reconciliation after separation	45	_____
Retirement	45	_____
Health problem of a close family member	44	_____

CHANGES	LCU's	SCORE
Pregnancy	40	_____
Difficulties with sex	39	_____
Arrival of a new family member	39	_____
Business readjustment	39	_____
Change in your personal financial state	38	_____
Death of a close friend	37	_____
Change in your line of work	36	_____
Increase in arguments with spouse	35	_____
Large mortgage taken out	31	_____
Foreclosure of mortgage or loan	30	_____
Change in work responsibilities	29	_____
Son or daughter leaving home	29	_____
Trouble with in-laws	29	_____
Major personal achievement	28	_____
Wife starting or stopping work	26	_____
Starting or leaving school	26	_____
Change in immediate living conditions	25	_____
Revision of personal habits	24	_____
Trouble with boss	23	_____
Change in work hours, residence, or schools	20	_____
Change in recreational or church activities	19	_____
Change in social activities	18	_____
Small mortgage taken out	17	_____
Change in sleeping habits	16	_____
Change in family get-togethers	15	_____
Change in eating habits	15	_____
Vacation	13	_____
Christmas	12	_____
Minor violations of the law	11	_____
TOTAL		_____

The LCU values are averages based on the reactions of a range of people, and therefore they are accurate only to the extent that you are an average person. In addition, the categories are not exhaustive, nor are they specific about details (your "trouble with the boss," for example, may be different from somebody else's). Nevertheless, the table does provide a way to assess statistically how stressful your life is. Holmes and Rahe, the originators of the system, suggest the following scale for interpreting your results. (The percentage figure indicates what proportion of Holmes and Rahe's respondents suffered an appreciable decline in health during the year in question.)

150 to 200	"Minor life crisis"	37%
200 to 300	"Moderate life crisis"	51%
Over 300	"Major life crisis"	79%

Spirituality

Spirituality is the last of the four major influences on physical health.

Numerous spiritual/psychological techniques are practiced in America today which help people achieve a state of deep relaxation. Yoga is an example. The Christian church has its own forms of prayer and biblical meditation which bring into play the same faculties of mind and spirit, and with a similar result. But in two ways the Christian finds *spirituality* and *health* to be far more intimately connected.

First, the health of the body is grounded in the health of the soul.

The Bible states categorically that all human beings are under the curse of sin, which means that from the spiritual point of view they are deprived of the thing they need most—union with God. In some mysterious way, the restoration of that union through Christ brings health not just to the spirit, but to the mind and body as well.

The very word *salvation* carries a Latin root—*salvus*—meaning "sound." As Psalm 16 puts it: "Because he [the Lord] is at my right hand, I shall not be moved. Therefore my heart is glad, and my soul rejoices; my body also dwells secure" (Psalm 16:8,9, RSV).

Second, God often steps in to restore physical health in response to faithful prayer: "He cured many people of their infirmities, afflictions, and evil spirits; and to many who were blind He gave sight," writes Luke (7:21).

I can testify myself to the reality of God's healing power. As a teenager, I should have lost a leg when a car I was in skidded and flipped over. Because of my parents' faithful prayer, I was healed and the surgeons didn't have to amputate.

The TOP Body

TRUST. If impossible health comes down to asking God's healing for an incurable condition, then the concept of *trust*—in God's ability and desire to bring wholeness—becomes the central issue. In the New Testament, James writes of the sick person: "Let him call for the elders of the church, and let them pray over him, anointing him with oil in the name of the Lord. And the prayer of faith will save the sick, and the Lord will raise him up. And if he has committed sins, he will be forgiven" (James 5:14,15). The use of the word "save" here (Greek *sozo*) reminds us of the wider concept of health espoused by the Christian. Though health is physical, and though God does often answer prayer for the restoration of the body, it is total health of body, mind, and spirit to which the Bible refers, and within which physical health is truly meaningful.

ORGANIZE. Trust expresses your confidence in the goal of physical fitness. Organization marshals the means by which that goal is reached. Assess the present impact on your body of the four major health influences. What kind of *nutrition* are you getting? Find out whether you're ingesting the full range of nutrients, and in the right quantities. How are you doing with *exercise*? Fitness will not be attained on less than four half-hour sessions a week. Are you under an unacceptable amount of *stress*? If so, track down the sources. And how long is it since you seriously examined the relationship between your health and your *spirituality*? Once you know where you are, do some research (seeking medical advice if necessary) then write a goals program that uses all four influences to bring you to physical fitness in not less than three months.

PERSIST. Physical health isn't a onetime goal. You don't achieve it and then go on to something else; health needs to be *maintained*. So when you've persisted to health, persist to keep it. Make health a habit.

15

INNER
HAPPINESS

Inner happiness is the most sought-after quality of human life. But many people find true happiness impossible to attain.

Everybody wants to be happy, and we've all had tantalizing glimpses of what complete happiness might be like. Unfortunately this was probably long ago, when we were too young to understand the world's miseries; when we fell in love; when financial blessing opened up new vistas of success and satisfaction before us; when the family last gathered together for Christmas.

These moments don't last. With the first setback our feeling that "all's right with the world" blows away, and we are left to chart our usual erratic course somewhere between hope and despondency. We can be truly happy, it seems, only as long as our circumstances are just right. Since most of the time our fortunes are mixed, happiness is forever retreating before the chill winds of anxiety. We're convinced that lasting happiness is an impossibility.

How Happy Are You?

Happiness is a complex thing.

Suppose I asked you to rate your happiness on a scale of one to ten. You'd probably reply by asking what I meant: happy right now, or happy in general? Happy about your investments, or happy about your daughter's wedding? People are almost always happy about some things and anxious about others. It's even possible to feel happy and anxious over the same thing at the same time—like the first day of a new job.

If we're going to actually measure happiness, we'll have to start by breaking life down into its different parts. The following table below uses 15 categories in three groups: *personal, relational,* and *contingent.* To use the table, assign each category two different percentages to indicate the greatest and the least happiness you derive from that particular area of your life. A scale is given to help you:

MEASURE YOUR HAPPINESS

100%	Ecstatic
90%	Very happy
80%	Happy
70%	Satisfied
60%	Moderately satisfied
50%	No feelings either way
40%	Slightly dissatisfied
30%	Dissatisfied
20%	Anxious
10%	Very anxious
0%	Frantic

CATEGORY	AT WORST	AT BEST
State of health:	%	%
Self-image:	%	%
Personal recreation time:	%	%
Sexuality:	%	%
Spiritual life:	%	%
Marriage:	%	%
Children:	%	%
Parents:	%	%
Close friendships:	%	%

Occupational environment— social:	%	%
Occupational environment— physical:	%	%
Home environment—physical:	%	%
Financial situation:	%	%
Occupational satisfaction:	%	%
Future prospects:	%	%

Three footnotes about the categories:

First, they are meant to be general. For example, "Occupation" can cover everything from management to motherhood.

Second, each can be interpreted negatively. In other words, you can measure the happiness or anxiety arising from *absence* of recreation time or *lack* of a spouse.

Third, the categories are meant to be realistic. Don't worry if you find yourself rating some area of your life 95 percent at best and 11 percent at worst. If that's the way you feel, say so.

Impossible Happiness?

The ideal situation is to have all your numbers well above 50 percent.

Is that impossible?

Not really. I know for a fact that using the TOP principles of Trust, Organization, and Persistence can revolutionize happiness. But you must understand two crucially important facts.

First, *happiness is available only to those who really want it.* I tell in another book (*How to Win Over Worry*) an experience of a pastor friend of mine, Eddie Lieberman. He was asked to help a young lady apparently suffering from severe depression. It turned out she had received a letter from her husband (who was overseas in the armed forces) telling her he had fallen in love with another girl and wanted a divorce. Eddie could have helped her come to terms with that problem, but she didn't want help, and by her mid-thirties her partially self-activated anxiety had turned her into a paralytic.

Second, *the idea that feeling must respond to circumstance is a myth*. That's a hard statement to accept, I know. We feel happy if we're loved and anxious if we're not, so doesn't that prove the power of circumstance over feeling? No, it doesn't, for the simple reason that what we *see* as circumstance isn't *real* circumstance at all. We exclude the wider picture.

That's why I cannot propose any solution to anxiety without reference to God. Read these words of the apostle Paul:

> Be anxious for nothing, but in everything by prayer and supplication, with thanksgiving, let your requests be made known to God; and the peace of God, which surpasses all understanding, will guard your hearts and minds through Christ Jesus (Philippians 4:6,7).

Let me summarize the matter briefly like this. Happiness is not attained by removing the causes of anxiety (they often can't be removed). Nor is it attained by pretending that the causes don't exist (they usually do exist). Happiness comes by allowing the presence of God to invade your perception and put the causes in their proper place. The Bible has a simple word for this process: *peace*. What the Bible says about finding peace can be summed up neatly in this formula:

PEACE = PRAISE + POISE + PRAYER

Peace Through Praise

In Philippians 4:4 Paul says, "Rejoice in the Lord always. Again I will say, rejoice!"

As a man who more than once had been stoned and left for dead, Paul knew what it was to praise God in adversity. He also knew that this method worked well. By a strange coincidence it was in Philippi that Paul and his companion, Silas, had been beaten up by the police and thrown into prison. Now Paul was human; nobody hears a cell door close behind him without feeling a surge of genuine anxiety. If the jailer had arrived the next morning to find Paul and Silas in a state of abject despair, we would hardly blame them for it. But they didn't give way to their feelings—they countered them. Luke says in Acts 16:25 that at midnight they were "praying and singing hymns to God." By their thoughts and actions they confronted and overcame the cause of their anxiety.

The same technique has been used by my close friend Bob Glaze. Bob has distinguished himself as a Bible teacher, a patron of the arts, a civic leader, a family man, a naval officer, and a businessman. He has been written up in the prestigious *Fortune* magazine. But he hasn't had things easy. When he quit his position as comptroller for a large organization to join three friends in starting a business, the venture collapsed within a year.

That might have finished a lesser man. But Bob understood Paul's attitude to anxiety, so he refused to panic or to grasp at the first opportunity that came along. Instead, he decided what he wanted to do and then set his mind on achieving the new goal. The target was America's leading developer, Trammell Crow of Dallas.

Bob had heard that Trammell Crow was a fitness buff. So at age 43 Bob got into top shape to prepare for an interview with Trammell. During the interview Trammell suggested visiting the fourteenth floor of one of his buildings. Bob had heard about the man's distaste for elevators, and when Trammell reached the fourteenth floor Bob was right behind him. Bob chuckles, recounting the experience: "I don't know if Trammell hired me because he thought I was a good man for the job or because he was impressed that I could stay with him up 14 flights of stairs!"

Don't make the mistake of thinking that praise has to do only with church attendance and worship. The attitude of praise should carry over into every area of your life, and especially into your treatment of other people. Anxious people are notorious for their dull conversation. They talk about nothing but their worries. They perpetually ask of other people an ear to listen and a shoulder to cry on. But this has the effect of reinforcing their own anxiety because they are forever reminding themselves of its causes.

Bear in mind some advice from Albert Schweitzer: "The only ones among you who will really be happy are those who have sought and found how to serve." Frank Tyger put it more succinctly: "If you want happiness, provide it to others."

Direct your attention outward. Offer to look after the children of a mother who has gotten sick. Offer to forward the mail for neighbors who are on vacation. Write a note of appreciation for your pastor.

From my visits to First Baptist Church in Cleveland, Tennessee, I remember a radiant 87-year-old called Uncle Joe Hawk. Uncle Joe's determined altruism would have warmed anyone's heart. During the depression, when his business as a drayman was feeling the pinch, he sold two of his best horses to keep the church afloat. It was a sacrifice which should have given him *more* to worry about, not less. But he gave for the joy of giving, and as far as I know he never got the money back, and never expected to.

Peace Through Poise

Poise is essential if you want to turn happiness into a practical possibility.

There were two farmers. One was a pessimist and the other was an optimist.

The optimist would say, "Wonderful sunshine!"

The pessimist would respond, "Yeah, I'm afraid it's going to scorch the crops."

The optimist would say, "Fine rain!"

The pessimist would respond, "Yeah, looks like we're going to have a flood."

One day the optimist said to the pessimist, "Have you seen my new bird dog? He's the finest money can buy."

The pessimist replied, "You mean that mutt I saw penned up behind your house? He don't look like much to me."

The optimist asked, "How about going hunting with me tomorrow?"

The pessimist agreed, so they went, and shot some ducks, which landed in a pond. The optimist ordered his dog to get the ducks, and the dog obediently responded. But instead of swimming in the water after the ducks, the dog walked on top of the water, retrieved the ducks, and walked back on top of the water.

The optimist turned to the pessimist and said, "Now what do you think of that?"

The pessimist replied, "Hmmm, he can't swim, can he?"

Pessimism is often hailed as gritty and realistic, but that's just not true. Pessimism is popular because unpleasant experiences make a greater impact on us than pleasant ones. The result is that we become obsessed with negativity in the mistaken belief that pessimism is the only rational response to our situation.

To find peace we must stop this mental deterioration in its early stages.

However bad the situation is, we will not be helped one iota by wallowing in anxiety. Our only hope lies in positive action undertaken in a positive frame of mind. Poise, then, begins by deliberately replacing anxious thoughts with happy ones. Paul writes: "Whatever things are true, whatever things are noble, whatever things are just, whatever things are pure, whatever things are lovely, whatever things are of good report, if there is any virtue and if there is anything praiseworthy—meditate on these things" (Philippians 4:8).

We can call this process "thought control." Edith Armstrong testifies that it works:

> I keep the telephone of my mind open to peace, harmony, health, love and abundance. Then, whenever doubt, anxiety or fear try to call me, they keep getting a busy signal—and they'll soon forget my number.[1]

Thought control is easier if you take time to relax. Having flown around the globe 63 times in the last 22 years, I think I am qualified to assure you that relaxation is both essential and possible.

In the early seventies I took a flight from Miami to Rio de Janeiro with a young colleague, Dr. Michael Youssef. After a long delay the plane finally left at 11 P.M. As we rumbled down the runway I said to Michael, "I'm going to turn this penlight on and do some reading."

I nodded off almost immediately. When I woke up we were still rumbling down the runway. "When in the world are we going to take off?" I said to Michael.

He rolled his eyes. "This is Caracas, Venezuela. You've been sleeping so hard since we left Miami, we couldn't even shake you awake for the meal."

Peace Through Prayer

Paul's teaching on happiness and anxiety is specifically

linked to prayer: "Be anxious for nothing, but in every-thing by prayer and supplication, with thanksgiving, let your requests be made known to God" (Philippians 4:6). Prayer results in two transformations.

First, there is a transformation of mind. In speaking to God you address yourself to the Person in whom all causes of anxiety have their resolution. The Bible makes it abundantly clear that we are given strength to rejoice in our difficulties if only we will receive it.

John Newton, the converted slave-trader and writer of the famous hymn *Amazing Grace*, put it like this:

> I compare the troubles which we have to undergo in the course of the year to a great bundle of fagots, far too large for us to lift. But God does not require us to carry the whole at once. He mercifully unties the bundle, and gives us first one stick, which we are to carry today, and then another, which we are to carry tomorrow, and so on. This we might easily manage, if we would only take the burden appointed for us each day; but we choose to increase our troubles by carrying yesterday's stick over again today, and adding tomorrow's burden to our load, before we are required to bear it.[2]

Second, there is a transformation of spirit. Anybody can pray, but nobody can pray and expect to be answered unless he comes to God in an attitude of weakness and repentance. You can't pull rank with God! Prayer does not bring God into line with your plans; it brings *you* into line with *His* plans. And that's good news, because discovering your place in God's plan—in other words, discovering your salvation—is the source of the deepest possible peace and happiness.

That experience has nothing to do with social status

or even with church attendance. After one Sunday night service when I was in the pastorate, one of the most respected members of my 3000-strong congregation came to me weeping uncontrollably. This lady attended practically every service; she taught Sunday school and was prominent in both the Training Union and the Women's Missionary Society; she was an exemplary church member. Yet in the next half-hour I was treated to one of the most sordid confessions of duplicity and sin I had ever heard. She had been in turmoil for 11 years. Her health was poor and she was under psychiatric care. It wasn't until that night, when she admitted her helplessness and cast herself wholly on God, that she received strength to live dynamically.

Have you had that transformation? If you want to make true happiness a possibility, you'll need it.

The TOP Relaxer

TRUST. Lasting happiness is possible only on the basis of trust in God, because it is God alone who gives "the peace that passes understanding." Without the assurance of that peace, obstacles may be too large to overcome. With it, mountains of anxiety can be uprooted and cast into the sea.

ORGANIZE. According to the Bible, peace is found in a life that combines *praise* and *poise* and *prayer*. The peace of God doesn't always remove the causes of anxiety, nor does it ask us to pretend that those causes don't exist. But it *does* equip us with the spiritual and emotional resources we need to live happily in spite of the difficulties we face. For a fuller explanation than I can give here of praise, poise, and prayer, please refer to my book *How to Win Over Worry*.

PERSIST. To be truly happy means to go on being happy. Yet, because happiness is attained by spiritual transformation and the action of the will, happiness, like the manna of the Old Testament, must be gathered fresh each day. Booker T. Washington captured something of this idea in the following words:

> I believe that any man's life will be filled with constant and unexpected encouragement if he makes up his mind to do his level best each day and as nearly as possible reach the high-water mark of pure and useful living.

16

STRENGTH IN BEREAVEMENT

My only son, Johnny, died in 1975 after 24 years of perpetual suffering.

He was brutalized at birth by a drunken doctor. He breathed only once every $2^1/_2$ minutes for the first three hours of his life, and then spent the rest of his life lying prone or sitting in a wheelchair. He never gained control of his limbs and never uttered more than a couple of half-recognizable words.

Despite all that, Johnny was a remarkable, gifted, and happy child. He brought joy and inspiration wherever he went. And he assisted me through many difficult periods in my ministry with his devoted prayer and patient, eager listening.

A short while before he was taken from us, I started to write a book. I called it *My Son Johnny*, and intended it as a tribute not just to Johnny but to my wife, Chris, who for so long had sacrificed herself for his sake. Reading back over it now I am struck by the final few lines:

> I like to think of our son in heaven, walking and running at last. What an enormous victory it must be for someone like him, to have been a lifelong prisoner in a body wracked with discomfort and pain and then to find release in the horizonless vistas of eternity!
>
> I miss him.
>
> Terribly, sometimes.

>But Johnny is free, free at last, and like his
>mother, I thank God.

More than a decade has passed since I wrote those words. I still miss him. The death of this person who is dear to me has left a lasting mark. He changed me. He turned me from a married man into a father, with all that this means. Now that he's gone, the change remains, reminding me of him—and of his absence.

Hurting's Okay

I tell you about Johnny because I want you to understand where I'm coming from. Having been bereaved myself, I can picture very easily what you're going through if you've lost someone who was close to you. It hurts. But I want you to know that hurting is okay, even if it hits you in unexpected ways.

For example, if you have lost someone you love recently, you will probably have experienced some of the following:

- A refusal to believe that it has happened.
- Feelings that the person you've lost is really still around.
- A desire to "look for" the person someplace where he or she used to go.
- An urge to talk to the person as if he or she were still there.
- A compulsion to talk to others about the person.
- Inability to talk at all.
- Bouts of unnatural determination to carry on as if nothing had happened.
- Violent changes in mood and sudden feelings of depression.
- Fits of uncontrollable weeping.

- Anger with God—for letting the death happen.
- Anger with the person who died—for abandoning you.
- Anger with other people—just for being happy.
- A desire to find somebody to pin the blame on.
- Guilt that somehow, because of the person you are, you deserved to be bereaved.
- Guilt that you failed to prevent the death from occurring.
- Guilt that you are still alive.
- A collapsing sensation, or even going completely to pieces so that other people have to look after you.
- A need to "replace" the person you've lost—with somebody else, with an activity, or perhaps even with overeating or undereating.

In terms of your usual behavior none of these reactions is normal. But then death is not a normal event. The abrupt removal of a person you have known and loved for a long time is about the worst blow you can be dealt. Your stability, your happiness, your future—all of these and more are suddenly and violently assaulted. Consequently you go into your own kind of shock.

All the symptoms of bereavement mentioned in the list above are aspects of that "shock reaction." They're as natural as bleeding from a wound, and they're designed, unconsciously, to help you cope with the fact of death. It's often said that the symptoms come in phases, so that a bereaved person moves, over several months, through a series of states of mind. That concept should not be pushed too far. Disbelief, for example, that should come somewhere near the beginning of the grief process, may crop up again years later.

The most you can say with certainty is this: However acute the pain is when a person you love dies, it does not last forever. Bereavements heal just like physical injuries. They may leave scars, but in the end they heal and let you return to an ordinary life. It's been my own experience that trust, organization, and persistence assist that healing. So I have no hesitation in assuring you that you can find strength in your bereavement.

You can get through it.

Understand What's Happening to You

Let me tell you a story that at first sight has little to do with bereavement, but it's tremendously illuminating.

Max Cleland was a young man in his early twenties when he volunteered for duty in Vietnam. He determined before he left that if he didn't return a hero he would at least—through faith and prayer—prove himself courageous. He didn't know then how much he would need that courage, or in what way.

It was one month from the scheduled end of his tour that the battle began for Khe Sanh. Not long after dawn, five days into battle, Max jumped out of a chopper and headed for the radio relay station. He saw a grenade at his feet. Thinking it had fallen off his own web gear, he reached to pick it up.

There was a blinding explosion.

Max was hurried out in a Med-Evac chopper and taken to a surgical hospital in Quang Tri, 40 miles away. He should have been dead. His right arm and both legs were gone. He had a shrapnel wound in his windpipe. He clung to life by sheer power of will.

For the next 18 months he was in and out of military hospitals. The ward he spent the most time in, at the Walter Reed Medical Center, was lovingly referred to by its occupants as the "Snake Pit." He lived surrounded by fellow amputees, unable to write and assured by the doctors that he would never walk again. He struggled to regain a sense of his manhood but doubted his prospects of survival. He was glad to be alive, but glad for little else.

One moment in particular focused the pain he felt. An old girlfriend came to see him, and they wheeled out into Washington D.C. to see the sights and have lunch. Approaching a crossing, however, the front wheels went down over the curb, and Max pitched forward out of the chair and into the gutter. As he later recalled in "Never Say Never":

> I flailed helplessly like a fish out of water, lying in the dirt and the cigarette butts. Two men rushed up from the growing crowd watching the mishap and lifted me back into the wheelchair.
>
> My companion was almost hysterical, repeatedly crying over and over, "I'm sorry, Max! I'm sorry!"
>
> We went on to lunch, but the shame and embarrassment of the spill seared me like a burn that continued to throb. I couldn't forget the first time I met her. I was 24 then, and I stood six feet two inches tall. Now I was in a wheelchair. I thought: "Is this all that's left for me—to be hauled around like a sack of potatoes for the rest of my life? No! I'm not always going to be helpless. I may need a lot of help from God, family, and friends, but I'm going to make a difference in this world."

And that's exactly what Max has done. Eventually he returned to his hometown in Lithonia, Georgia, to a hero's welcome. He relearned to walk with the help of artificial limbs supplied by the Veterans Association, relearned to drive by adapting his car, and set up his own apartment, living an independent, "abled" life. In 1970 he ran successfully for the Georgia State Senate. Since then he has gone on to occupy a staff position on the U.S. Senate Committee on Veterans' Affairs and to serve two terms as Secretary of State for Georgia.

Bereavement, Loss, and Healing

Max Cleland's story has much to teach us about trust, organization, and persistence.

But it also casts an important sidelight on bereavement. That's why I've chosen to tell it here. Loss of a limb and loss of a loved one are strikingly similar. Both involve the breaking of a previous wholeness; both demand a massive readjustment to new circumstances; both push the victim into a process of grief. In fact, people who have lost a person they love often use the metaphor of amputation: "We were so close it seemed like we were part of each other," they'll say, or: "It's like a bit of me has been cut off."

To be "close" to someone is to give away a large share of your time, your attention, and your love, and to create mutual dependence in areas such as food, relaxation, ownership, family responsibility, and emotional support. In that sense even a pet can become "part of you" and cause you to grieve at its death.

So where does healing begin?

Probably right alongside bereavement. The Bible supplies a helpful insight in the second book of Samuel. Having committed adultery with Bathsheba, and having arranged for her husband to be killed, David is confronted by the prophet Nathan and forewarned that in punishment for his sin the child which Bathsheba has conceived will die. The child is born, and shortly thereafter gets sick.

David's response is to pray. For seven days he refuses to eat and lies at night on the bare ground. When the child dies, the servants are so fearful of what David will do that they hesitate to tell him. David, however, overhears their whispers and demands to be told the truth. His reactions surprised everyone:

> So David arose from the ground, washed and anointed himself, and changed his clothes;

and he went into the house of the Lord and worshiped. Then he went to his own house; and when he requested, they set food before him, and he ate.

Then his servants said to him, "What is this that you have done? You fasted and wept for the child while he was alive, but when the child died, you arose and ate food."

So he said, "While the child was still alive, I fasted and wept; for I said, 'Who can tell whether the Lord will be gracious to me, that the child may live?' But now he is dead; why should I fast? Can I bring him back again? I shall go to him, but he shall not return to me."

Then David comforted Bathsheba his wife, and went in to her and lay with her. So she bore a son, and he called his name Solomon. And the Lord loved him (2 Samuel 12:20-24).

The passage might seem to imply a tidy end to David's grief, but almost certainly, as we see from the last verse, the grieving continued long after the child died. What we are shown, though, is a corner that nearly every grieving person turns, a corner at which looking forward starts to become more important than looking back.

Traveling Through Bereavement

Bereavement is like a journey: We are traveling from a place of happiness where we once thought we could live forever, but which has been destroyed by the death of a person we love. We can live there no longer. We are on the road, feeling lost, searching for another place of happiness to make our home. Sometimes it seems as though no such place exists. Yet, at some point along the road, we look up and realize we have turned the corner. Far ahead on the horizon we glimpse a destination that feels like home. It is not the same place of happiness we left, nor do we believe it can make us as happy as we once were, but still it lies within our reach. We want to get there.

How rough the journey of bereavement is depends on many things. The trauma of grief is greater with those you're close to. Loss of a husband or wife, in whom you have made a heavy emotional and material investment, in all probability will hit you harder than loss of a parent from whom you've been independent for 20 years.

Be aware also that while family and friends are a tremendous support in bereavement, they may not always be able to understand what you're going through. I expect you've already been encouraged to "pull yourself together," or admonished for not being "over that stage by now." Six months after a death most people will expect you to be back on top of the world. They don't realize that the journey of bereavement often takes two years.

To a large extent bereavement is survived through hope—hope in the fact that it will come to an end, and that you will, in the not-too-distant future, reach another place of happiness to make your own. Having said that, though, I must add a few hints to help you as you travel.

BEREAVEMENT: A TRAVELER'S GUIDE

1. *Let go of the one you love.* Death is a parting of the ways. You can no longer care for the person who has died; whether you like it or not, you're forced to give him or her into the care of God.

   That can be painful. It's against your instincts to yield to the fact of death. But yielding is in the end the only way to leave death behind. That is why the formal farewells of a funeral are so important, and why acceptance of death is so much more of a problem when no bodily remains can be found, or when the person has died in a distant place and seems to be still only "away from home."

2. *Affirm the past through thanksgiving.* Especially when death is premature, the person's past life will seem darkened by irony and injustice. His achievements will shrink to insignificance beside the monstrous waste of potential brought about by his death. And yet, even if the one you love didn't die like Abraham, "old and full of years," it is important that his living be remembered more than his dying. Such blessing as you received through him—and you will have received a lot—remains blessing even as it recedes into the past. Treasure your memories, then, and give thanks to God for what you were given.

3. *Take encouragement from scripture.* The Bible is full of comfort for the bereaved. Read the Psalms and you will find, alongside the praise to God, a real familiarity with pain and suffering. Read the Gospels and you will meet again the Savior in whom, as Paul wrote later, "death has been swallowed up in victory." In prayer you may well feel a sense of God's remoteness. That's understandable. But don't worry—you will find comfort and strength in His Word.

4. *Allow others to help you.* Try not to isolate yourself. There are plenty of people around who want to share the burden of your grief: pastors, counselors, family, and friends. Being with them will lift your spirits and help you to cope.

   Faithful as friends are, they may not find your bereavement any easier to handle than you do. Sometimes they don't know what to say, and may appear awkward for fear of saying something that will hurt your feelings. If that's the case, "allowing others to help" might mean being honest with them about the way you feel so they don't put their foot in their mouths.

5. *Be gently disciplined.* There are times when we all need to lean on others. As far as possible, however, try to

keep the externals of your life moving at the usual pace. If you're a mother of small children, that will be necessary for their sake. But it will also give you a reassurance that life has not completely fallen apart, and will occupy your attention at a time when long periods of inactivity could be depressing.

A Grief Observed

It is *trust in God* that makes the greatest difference in bereavement.

Being a Christian doesn't exempt you from pain, but it does put a few breaks in the cloud overhead. After all, a believer who dies is not lost—he has gone to be in the nearer presence of God, and so on his account, at least, there is no reason to be sad.

I can think of no finer example of faith in God in time of bereavement than Bishop Wayan Mastra, who lost one of his children in tragic circumstances. He and his wife went through many of the symptoms of grief I outlined earlier in the chapter, but in the end they discovered that their loss taught them a profound lesson. Since I can add nothing to the story, I'm going to let Wayan Mastra speak for himself.

> My wife and I had four lovely daughters. They were loved and cared for in our happy family. But one day disaster struck. While playing on the beach, under supervision, our small, six-year-old daughter Ketut was suddenly swept up by a large freak wave and carried out to sea. All attempts to reach her failed and her body was never recovered.
>
> Why did this terrible thing happen? All around us other children, neglected and abused, lived on while our precious daughter was taken from us.
>
> It was an enormous struggle for the whole family to come to terms with this loss. It was like an amputation, losing a healthy limb from the family tree, and we were left hurting badly.

But even through this desperate feeling of separation from someone loved, someone whose potential had been so cut off, we knew that we had a resource in our faith in God which would bring us through this black tunnel of grief.

Our personal tragedy took us right back to the very basis of our faith. We had to relearn to trust that God's purpose for us, even though so seemingly defeated or mocked, was always for our eventual good.

This trust in God went as deep as reaffirming our conviction that all belongs to Him—the very air we breathe, the family we create, all possessions and the whole of the life we live. In the ultimate sense we own nothing—all belongs to God. Our response is to use our lives, with their joys and sorrows, as responsibly as we can.

Thus we were able to release our treasured daughter into the loving arms of God, her heavenly Father, whose child she really was. We have a saying in Bali, *"angkian baan nyilih,"* which means "life comes from borrowing." So we knew that God welcomed back His child.

Also we learned that nothing happens in isolation. Our tragedy enabled us to understand the suffering of other people. It had opened a gateway through which we walked into an enlarged world of human sympathy, compassionate caring, and intercessory prayer for all those people whose lives have been interrupted by unwanted sorrow. We now know how heavy is the burden of grieving people, for we have shouldered the load ourselves.

Throughout, we were and are perpetually reminded that God Himself went through it all for us. We know He shares in our suffering because He Himself endured the agony of Christ on the cross. So we know that He will give us the strength to surmount our grief.

We learned that God's way for us is through sorrow to victory.

The TOP Survivor

TRUST. In her famous book *On Death and Dying*, Dr. Elisabeth Kubler-Ross wrote: "Once the patient dies, I find it cruel and inappropriate to speak of the love of God." Nevertheless, His love remains. Hard though it may be to see Him, God goes with us through every suffering, and gives us hope that sooner or later we will turn the corner in our journey of bereavement and see an end. "The very hairs of your head are all numbered. Do not fear therefore" (Luke 12:7).

ORGANIZE. I've implied by using the analogy of a journey that the landscape of bereavement is fixed and unchangeable—that, like it or not, everybody goes through much the same experience. But while the loss of someone you love carries with it a familiar and well-documented upheaval, the situation isn't entirely beyond your control. You can begin to organize yourself in a way that makes the passage easier. Five priorities are particularly helpful:

1. Let go of the one you love.
2. Affirm the past through thanksgiving.
3. Take encouragement from Scripture.
4. Allow others to help you.
5. Be gently disciplined.

PERSIST. Remember that grieving takes time. You can help it, but you can't hurry it. Don't be despondent if 12 months afterward you're still missing your husband, your wife, your parent, your child, or your friend. And don't be afraid to ask for help. If you've ever had major surgery you remember that you went back to the hospital numerous times for checkups.

You *can* find strength in bereavement. Keep moving in the midst of grief. Eventually you'll leave it behind.

A Personal Postscript

Just days before writing this chapter, my father died. We all knew it was coming. He and I discussed his home-going at length. He wanted to go. I had no idea I would suffer such a jolt after his departure. In comparing my emotional diary with my brother Tom's, we found that our experiences were similar.

We wouldn't call him back even if we had the power to do so. But there is the painful void left in our lives. I still find myself grabbing for the telephone to get his idea on some matter; then before dialing I realize he is no longer here.

Tom and I independently concluded that the way we would resolve this bereavement would be to replicate Dad's personal discipline. He was disciplined in his devotions. He spent time in prayer every morning. He read the Bible through 103 times in the course of his life. He was disciplined in his exercise. He considered it sinful for anyone not to take care of his body. He was disciplined in his eating habits. He was disciplined in his commitments. He missed Sunday School only one time in nearly 70 years.

Tom and I believe there is real benefit to be derived emotionally in the pursuit of Dad's disciplined lifestyle.

MAXIMUM MATURITY

It's possible for your years after 65 to be the best—the most productive and the most satisfying.

Benjamin Franklin was ambassador to France when he was 83; William E. Gladstone was prime minister of England at 83; Konrad Adenauer was chancellor of West Germany at 87; Deng Xiaoping was chairman of the Communist Party Central Advisory Commission at 83; Verdi wrote operas in his 90's; Paul Dudley White, famous Boston cardiologist, achieved even greater international prominence in his 80's. Somerset Maugham continued to create until age 92; Vladimir Nabokov was writing at peak form in his late 70's; Carl Sandburg and Robert Frost produced poetry well into their 80's; Armand Hammer retired as he neared 80 and then built the Occidental Petroleum Corporation. Grandma Moses began her career in art at 72; Thomas Edison remained active and productive until 83.

I enjoy visiting with Mr. A.V. Kennedy in Waycross, Georgia, who at the time of this writing is 101 years old. He still drives his car, conducts his affairs, and demonstrates an alertness that holds me in awe.

Playwright Garson Kanin was right, "It takes a long time to become young!"

But this isn't a chapter only for the over-65's.

It's for anyone who feels that he or she has already seen the best in life, and looks ahead without relish to what seems to be a second-rate future. That feeling can hit you at 45 if you're a man and at 35 if you're a woman.

Suddenly things you've taken for granted (good looks, energy, career prospects, a full head of hair) start to slip away from you, and you start thinking not about how *many* good years are left, but how *few*.

That sense of loss is unnerving. It isn't just a matter of poorer health or diminished status. You wonder if you haven't lost forever the opportunity to do things you had always dreamed of doing. It's a loss of hope.

Getting more out of your remaining years than you've gotten from the ones behind you seems impossible. Yet there's no reason why that should be the case. Scores of my maturer friends, both men and women, see a long life ahead, filled with vigorous and fulfilling achievement. They would agree with Swift that "no wise man ever wished to be younger."

Trust, organization, and persistence are vital to coping with your progress through life. At every stage there are turning points—leaving college, starting a family, changing jobs. Midlife crisis and the approach to maturity are also turning points. They give us a chance to pause and ask ourselves where we're going. We pull over and consult the map. That pause for thought is the key to overcoming the fear and emptiness that plague many people as they search for a "maximum maturity."

Life Location

Figure 17.1 is called the Life Location Chart. You can use it to find out where you are in the story of your life.

This story is not the one told about you by other people—employers, friends, doctors, or financial advisers—but the one you tell yourself. It is an unbroken narrative, the kind that begins at the beginning and ends at the end. That is why the bottom axis of the chart is measured in years. The side axis is more personal. During your life so far you will have experienced a number

Figure 17.1: The Life Location Chart

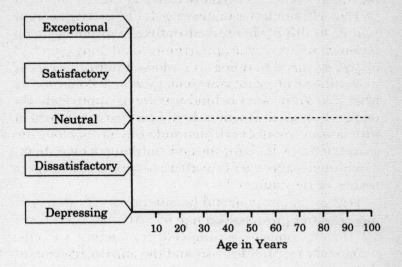

Life Corners:

A _____

B _____

C _____

D _____

E _____

F _____

G _____

of *life corners*—events memorable to you because they mark especially high or low (or perhaps just especially significant) events. These may vary in type (graduation, marriage, conversion, and promotion are all common *life corners*), but they can all be measured in terms of how "good" or "bad" they seem to you as you look back on them.

To use the chart, begin by measuring the present moment, and marking your score with an X. Then decide what your *life corners* are and enter them chronologically on the chart with the letters A, B, C, and so on. Join them with a wavy curve to indicate how life has gone in the spaces between. Finally, when the curve arrives at the X, continue it to the end of the chart to suggest your expectations of the future.

Age, the Distant Horizon

What the Life Location Chart does is collect the sometimes-quite-vague feelings you have about the way your life is going, and puts them into a single pattern. Now take a look at Figure 17.2, which shows how two different people might fill in the chart.

Mr. Hoyt is 32. The focal point of his youth is his desire to become a lawyer. Failing to enter law school is therefore his first *life corner*. Soon after that he meets his wife-to-be. He scores his wedding as slightly better than satisfactory, and his married life as slightly less.

Ms. Pecora scores her first wedding (when she was 19) as neutral. She has an unfulfilling marriage, deterioration setting in during her mid-twenties, and divorce coming about five years later. After that, though, she records two highly positive events. A move to a new job in a new city is followed quickly by a new, and apparently lasting, relationship. At age 58 she is still on a genuine high.

Figure 17.2: Two Imaginary Life Locations

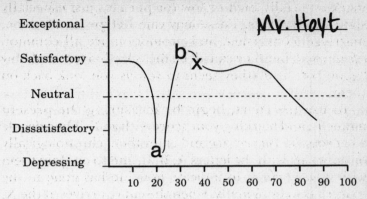

Mr. Hoyt

A <u>Failed Law School entrance</u>
B <u>Married Kate</u>

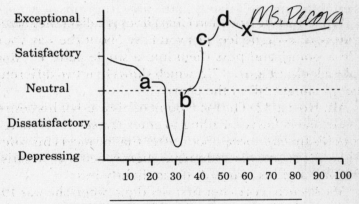

Ms. Pecora

A <u>Marriage</u>
B <u>Divorce</u>
C <u>Got job in San Francisco</u>
D <u>Met Joseph</u>

Notice how these two people see the future. While Mr. Hoyt hopes for some improvement toward the end of his career, he is pessimistic about retirement. Ms. Pecora, on the other hand, already extremely happy, forecasts at least another 30 years, each a little better than the last.

Only half a century ago, Mr. Hoyt's glum forecasts might have been more realistic. Life expectancy was shorter, and the quality of life enjoyed by older people was far lower than it is today. For many people a happy, fulfilling existence did not stretch far beyond age 65. Now this is becoming the exception and not the norm. It's no longer unusual for older people to remain fit and active into their eighties and even into their nineties. Consequently the old French dictum that life has three ages—of growing, working, and living—is taking on new significance. The Third Age, anticipated by Ms. Pecora, is establishing itself firmly in the life-programs of America, and "age" in the previous sense of frailty and senility is receding toward the horizon.

Leisure for What?

But what are we going to do with the Third Age now that we have it?

It's not difficult to find impressive examples of achievement by people who might justifiably be resting on their laurels:

- Havergal Brian didn't compose a symphony until he was 80. He liked it so much that he composed another 17 before he died at 93.

- Roy Thompson, former owner of *The Times* newspaper of London, moved his company into the British North Sea Oil Industry when he was 77.

- Australian Sir Bruce Small served simultaneously as member of Parliament, Mayor of
  the Gold Coast, and head of the largest property development company in Queensland.
  He also made the *Guinness Book of Records* as
  the oldest man ever to initially run for an
  elective office in politics and win. He was 76
  at the time.

But not everyone uses the Third Age so constructively.
Strangely, in fact, one of the impossibilities of maturity
today can be finding something worthwhile to do with it.
This is (sometimes literally) fatal. But it arises naturally
out of a certain life-stance.

When British Prime Minister Benjamin Disraeli said,
"Youth is a blunder, manhood a struggle, age a regret,"
he reflected what is still true for countless men and
women today. Ineffectual middle age slowly gives way to
a slack, introspective maturity, with nothing better to
occupy it than self-pity and an occasional round of golf.

I believe that a large part of the problem here lies in
the concept of retirement. To retire means, literally,
to draw back from. Retire from what? From work, presumably. And yet work is probably the most important
element in the chemistry of life. Hans Selye, the original
authority on stress, writes:

> Work is a biological necessity. Just as our
> muscles become flabby and degenerate if not
> used, so our brain slips into chaos and confu-
> sion unless we constantly use it for some work
> that seems worthwhile.[1]

Dr. Ernest H. Watson took on the herculean responsibility of deanship at Haggai Institute at the age of 66.
No one, including myself, could match his dedication at
the training sessions. He sat through every period from

start to finish. Immediately after his quiet time in the morning, he would plunge into the pool and swim 50 laps before men half his age were even awake. Between sessions he would write, counsel, travel, preach, screen applicants, and report to donors. I remember one time a participant telling me it was "inhuman" for Haggai Institute to impose its seven-to-nine program every day for five or six weeks. And he was only 36! I'm glad to say that Dr. Watson's example made as much impact on this young man's leadership development as the course itself.

Don't misunderstand me—I'm not recommending workaholism. You overcome the impossibility in maturity by the same careful balance of work and leisure that applies at every stage of life. And leisure itself, of course, is not simply the *opposite* of work, but its *complement*. In their book *Must Success Cost So Much?* Paul Evans and Fernando Bartolome see leisure as four-sided.[2] I have adapted the "four sides" as follows:

FOUR SIDES TO LEISURE

1. *Leisure as recovery.* This involves easy, largely solitary activities like watching TV, doing odd jobs, sunbathing, and snoozing. We use this form of leisure when we're tired and need recuperation.

2. *Leisure as relaxation.* This more active kind of leisure, popular among managers and professionals, uses a sport or hobby to clear the mind and train the body.

3. *Leisure as family investment.* Holidays, outings, barbecues, picnics, and games allow a family to enjoy leisure together. It functions as relaxation while also strengthening emotional bonds.

4. *Leisure as personal development.* This form of leisure takes relaxation into learning. In resting, therefore, you are able to gain expert skill which may be useful in the work situation.

Preparing for Act Two

If you want to transform impossibility at any major turning point in life, it's worth investing a little time in reviewing your goals. How far have you achieved what you set out to do? Have circumstances knocked your goal-setting program off course? What new priorities have come into play that should be built into your existing goals pattern?

One method of going about this reappraisal is to use the survey below. It invites you to categorize your past and present goals. This enables you to see at a glance what your goals structure is, then to check each individual goal for its present status. Thus a goal can be:

1. (U) Unimportant for you personally
2. (A) Already achieved
3. (C) Continuously achieved
4. (N) Not yet achieved

A TEN-POINT GOAL SURVEY

1. Leadership:

_____
_____ U / A / C / N
_____ U / A / C / N
_____ U / A / C / N
_____ U / A / C / N

2. Expertness:

_____
_____ U / A / C / N
_____ U / A / C / N
_____ U / A / C / N
_____ U / A / C / N

3. Service:

_____

_____ U / A / C / N
_____ U / A / C / N
_____ U / A / C / N
_____ U / A / C / N

4. Finance:

_____

_____ U / A / C / N
_____ U / A / C / N
_____ U / A / C / N
_____ U / A / C / N

5. Independence:

_____

_____ U / A / C / N
_____ U / A / C / N
_____ U / A / C / N
_____ U / A / C / N

6. Relationship:

_____

_____ U / A / C / N
_____ U / A / C / N
_____ U / A / C / N
_____ U / A / C / N

7. Personal development:

_____

_____ U / A / C / N
_____ U / A / C / N
_____ U / A / C / N
_____ U / A / C / N

8. Church involvement/spirituality:

_____	U / A / C / N
_____	U / A / C / N
_____	U / A / C / N
_____	U / A / C / N

9. Adventure:

_____	U / A / C / N
_____	U / A / C / N
_____	U / A / C / N
_____	U / A / C / N

10. Enjoyment:

_____	U / A / C / N
_____	U / A / C / N
_____	U / A / C / N
_____	U / A / C / N

The Ski's the Limit!

I hope you have a lot of major goals marked "A," as well as many others (such as maintaining a good family life) that still deserve a "C." Take a look at the "U's" and the "N's." Are the areas you considered unimportant ten years ago still unimportant now? Do you think you were right to consider them unimportant in the first place? As for the goals not yet achieved, have you had them for a long time? If so, why haven't you achieved them? Is the program in need of restructuring?

I find the previously unimportant goals demand more attention as I get older. At the age of 62 I decided to make a goal out of something I had always wanted to do but somehow, in my younger years, had never gotten around to: I decided to learn downhill skiing.

Determined to achieve this apparently impossible goal, I called John Bolten, a friend who lives in Germany.

"Skiing? Are you serious?"

"Yes, Now what do I do?"

"Get an instructor."

"Where?"

"Austria. The best ski instructors are Austrian."

So I set aside time for a vacation in the Austrian Alps. I can't say that my friends were unanimous in their support for the venture. "Your muscle tone isn't what it used to be, John," one counseled me. "If you get on the ski slope, you'll be going so slow that some speedy downhill skier will hit you like you're a brick wall." Another added, "You'll doubtlessly break a leg."

This prompted another call to John Bolten.

"Get your legs in shape, John. It's important that your legs be in first-class shape."

So I adopted a training program that was part physical and part psychological. For 30 minutes each morning I sweated it out on my Air Dyne Schwinn bicycle until my legs were stronger than they had been for years. At the same time I used positive affirmations. "You've got the genes," I told myself. "Your father played tennis till he was 85. Your grandfather competed in ice-skating contests on Charles River in Boston when he was older than you are. It'll be good for your rapport with the young and increase your credibility. You can learn to downhill ski. In fact it's your responsibility to do it."

I read the right books. I watched the right TV programs. I asked the right questions. I went to see the right specialists for medical advice. Finally, 12 months after my first call to John Bolten, I arrived in Austria, complete with an entourage of friends and family. It wasn't the greatest performance the Austrian Alps have ever seen, but it was respectable. I achieved my goal.

The TOP Senior

TRUST. Maturity is one of life's turning points. As such, it isn't the signal to start shutting down the system so you can coast gently downhill. Just like other turning points, it offers new and unique opportunities for achievement. In fact, as the Third Age, it may offer opportunities you have never had before.

You can make maturity work for you, just as it worked for Moses, whose "eyes were not dim nor his natural vigor abated" (Deuteronomy 34:7) though he lived to be 120 years old. There is no reason for you to conform to stereotypes which belong to a previous generation. Your grandfather may have hit the rocking chair at 65, but will you?

ORGANIZE. The secret of achieving the impossible in maturity is to understand that the same rules apply at 70 as at 40. You still need that balance of leisure and work. They may or may not be different in detail—that depends on your own particular goals program. But make sure you review the program, bringing in new goals as old ones are achieved.

PERSIST. My father read the Bible from cover to cover over a hundred times. That's one of the repeated short-term goals that gave him vision and purpose through to his nineties. Look on it as a deal. You support your goals, they will support you. Long may it continue!

18

NO EXCUSES

"All things," said Jesus, "are possible to him who believes" (Mark 9:23).

I'm sure you've read that verse many times and bathed in the warmth of its assurance. Of course, God is the God of the miraculous. He can do anything. All things are possible.

But as a believer, have you fully comprehended what God is saying? Jesus wasn't stating some elegant divine principle with no earthly application. When He said that all things are possible, He meant that all things are possible _for you_.

Let that soak in.

Ponder again the circumstances that moved you to pick up a copy of this book. Could it be you are looking for a way to deal with some seeming impossibility in your life? Maybe you've got relationship trouble—difficult kids, a rocky marriage, no one to love you. Maybe you have dreams of exercising leadership, boosting your income, recovering from some catastrophic failure, or achieving great things in church growth, evangelism, or giving. Maybe your particular impossibility is related to being mature, or being a woman, or to the quest for health and happiness. Maybe you have some crazy dream all your own that you never thought you could realize.

Now say to yourself: "All things are possible. All things are possible for me _because God says so_."

Is there any reason why you shouldn't live from now on in the light of that promise? Don't just agree without thinking. Maybe you can think of plenty of reasons—reasons that have dominated your outlook for years and will come back to haunt you as soon as you hit a setback. Here are some with which you may identify:

- "I don't have the time."
- "I know it can't be done."
- "It's too risky—I might get hurt."
- "Nothing I do will make any difference."
- "I'd only make a fool of myself."
- "I'd be causing other people inconvenience."
- "It's not my job."
- "I've tried it before and failed."
- "I don't know if God wants me to."
- "I know I don't have the ability."
- "Only pride makes me want to do it anyway."
- "No one else has done it, so why should I?"
- "There are other people better than I."
- "Too many people are against me."
- "I don't have enough money."
- "Nobody would believe I can do it."
- "I'd be better doing it next year."
- "It's beyond my control."
- "I have too much to lose."
- "I'm not well enough."
- "I shouldn't have to do this anyway."
- "I'm being pushed into it by others."
- "It's my fault I'm in a mess—I should take the consequences."

- "I can't make up my mind."
- "I'm not sure I want to."

Most of these reasons are valid for day-to-day purposes. All of us, myself included, reject certain options because they're risky, ineffective, or unpopular. But we're not talking about the day-to-day. We're talking about the *really important* things, the impossibilities that hurt and restrict us in a big way. And for giving up on those only one reason is good enough:

> "I'm absolutely sure God *doesn't* want me to do it."

If you can't say that, you're making excuses.

Don't get me wrong; I know it's tough for you, and I'm not belittling your problem. But I urge you to take God's promises to you seriously. You can turn the impossible into the possible.

All you need to succeed are the three elements of the TOP principle: **TRUST**—in yourself, in others, and supremely in God; **ORGANIZATION**—that identifies clear objectives and works toward them using well-conceived goal programs; and **PERSISTENCE**—without which no great work in the history of humankind has been brought to completion. Robert Half, quoted in *Forbes* magazine, put it simply: "The price of success is perseverance. Failure comes cheaper."

I know hundreds of people who have proved it.

The Doctor Who Wouldn't Give Up

The title of this book could be chiseled on the cornerstone of the Cooper Clinic and Aerobics Center buildings in Dallas, Texas. Every visitor I take to the 30-acre, 25-million-dollar property is smitten with the beauty of this internationally famous wellness center. I told one of them recently about its founder, Dr. Kenneth H. Cooper.

"He must have come from wealth to build a colossus like this in less than 20 years," my friend commented.

"No," I replied. "He didn't have dollars. He had a dream."

I told him the story.

Cooper was a career military officer, a flight surgeon. He had risen to the rank of Lieutenant Colonel, soon to be commissioned full Colonel, when at age 40 he resigned to enter the field of wellness and preventive medicine.

It was a hard decision. His wife, Millie, was pregnant, and he had no financial backing for the new enterprise. A Dallas city father, a multimillionaire, denied Cooper his 1.2-million-dollar request.

"Stay in the Air Force another seven years," he advised. "Don't risk giving up your benefits."

The reasons were mounting as to why Cooper should stay put. Yet when he and his wife prayed, they concurred that it was the Lord's leading.

There was no lending agency willing to put up more than 100,000 dollars, since Cooper's net worth was less than 25,000 dollars. But the young doctor persisted. Finally Joe McKinney, President of the Tyler Corporation, agreed to make a loan of 1.2 million.

I'm sure Joe McKinney feels a wave of satisfaction today when he thinks about the thousands, maybe millions, of people who have benefited from Cooper's philosophy. At that time, though, the obstacles for Cooper seemed to proliferate daily. Some respected Dallas doctors scoffed at his idea. He was called before the Dallas County Board of Censors to defend his position. Some medical men were pressing to restrict his practice, and even fractured the truth about him, claiming that he had been dishonorably discharged from military service and only had a Ph.D.

Had Cooper wanted to give up at this stage, he would have had no shortage of excuses. But he and his wife were certain that God had called them. So they prayed and persisted until the impossible was accomplished.

Their original vision had been for a modest office employing eight or ten people, but that goal was dramatically surpassed. Today his staff numbers 220. Adherents to Cooper's wellness philosophy live and work in 50 nations. His books have sold more than 17 million copies in 39 languages. Even as I write these words one of them is number 4 on the *New York Times* bestseller list.

The Cooper Clinic and Aerobics Center are the focal points of attention for medical, sports, and educational leaders from nations on every continent, including those behind the Iron Curtain. World leaders—among them medical men—come to him for their annual physical checkups. Only out of deference to their right to privacy do I refrain from naming some. Suffice it to say, hardly a day goes by when their names aren't in the news.

Today Dr. Kenneth H. Cooper continues to embody this book's formula—trust, organize, persist. He is a man of God, in a marriage made by God. His wife, Millie, shares his trust in God and his determination to see his goals achieved. Talk about organization! I have never been to any offices where things run more smoothly or promptly. The entire operation is a model of organizational excellence. Persistence? His annual budget today is more than ten times McKinney's original investment.

The TOP Succeeder

Dr. Cooper's is a big success story. It measures what can be done when somebody decides to trust, organize, and persist.

Of course his impossibility isn't the same one you're facing. But can you honestly say it was easier for Dr. Cooper than it is for you? Do you really have any more right than he to make excuses? Are you content to wallow in helplessness when other people, in situations as hard as yours, have managed to turn impossibility into possibility? Most important, do you think Jesus was joking when He said all things are possible to you if you believe?

No?

Then be careful what you call IMPOSSIBLE!

EPILOGUE

I dedicated this book "To the spirit of Waddy Abraham Haggai within each one of us waiting to be awakened."

Here's an example of that spirit. The week before Dad was rushed by ambulance to the hospital, his pastor, Dr. J. Hoffman Harris, visited him.

"Come in, beloved Shepherd (Dad's favorite title for his pastor)," Dad called out.

Throughout his professional life Dad's habit was to study while standing at a podium. On this day, however, his body no longer allowed him to do this. While reclining in a chair and the open Bible in his lap, he said to his minister, "I don't have a clear understanding of this passage, and I'm studying the Arabic translation to see if it casts any light on these verses."

Dr. Harris shook his head in disbelief. Here was a man who had read the Bible through 103 times, taught it for 75 years, and despite his excruciating pain, was digging into a biblical passage for a clearer understanding.

Dad was very careful what he called impossible. Nearly 27 years after the commonly accepted retirement age, Dad was still learning, teaching, working.

God bless you. Be careful what you call impossible.

NOTES

Chapter 1

1. The item headings S-M-A-R-T on pages 26-28 are from Paul J. Meyer, founder of Success Motivation Institute. The paragraphs under these are from Dr. Haggai.

Chapter 2

1. Winston Churchill quote in Lorraine Marshall and Francis Rowland, *A Guide to Learning Independently* (Milton Keyes: Open University Press, 1983), p. 190.
2. Adapted from Anne Howe, *Learn How to Study* (London: Kogan Page, 1986), pp. 46-47.
3. Ibid., p. 58.

Chapter 3

1. F. Scott Fitzgerald, *The Great Gatsby* (London: Penguin Modern Classics, 1964). Copyright held by F. Scott Fitzgerald estate.
2. Ted Engstrom and Robert Larson, *The Fine Art of Friendship* (Nashville: Thomas Nelson, 1985).
3. Jack Dominion, *Marriage, Faith and Love* (London: Fount Paperbacks, 1984), p. 95.

Chapter 4

1. James Dobson, *Parenting Isn't for Cowards* (Waco, TX: Word Publishing), p. 12.
2. Ann Landers in *Family Circle*, Nov. 3, 1981.

Chapter 5

1. Dominion, op. cit., p. 95.
2. Engstrom, op. cit.

Chapter 6

1. W.C.H. Prentice, *Harvard Business Review*, 1961.

Chapter 8

1. Henry Ford II quote from John Adair, *Management and Morality* (England: David and Charles Holdings Ltd., 1974).
2. Ibid.

Chapter 10

1. Gail Sheehy, *Passages* (New York: Bantam Books, 1977).
2. Mary Crowley, *You Can Too* (Old Tappan, NJ: Fleming H. Revell, 1980), pp. 16, 44.
3. Aristotle, *The Generation of Animals*, trans. A.L. Peck (London: Heinemann, 1943).

Chapter 12

1. Basil Mathews, *John R. Mott, World Citizen* (New York and London: Harper & Brothers, 1934), Prologue.

Chapter 14

1. Jack Foster, *Tale of the Ancient Marathoner,* quoted in *AAA Running Guide* (New York: Collins, 1983), p. 138.
2. Holmes-Rahe Analysis as worded in Trevor Martin, *Good Health* (London: Marshall Pickering, 1983), pp. 60-61.

Chapter 15

1. Edith Armstrong quote from *The Forbes Scrapbook of Thoughts on the Business of Life* (New York: Forbes, Inc., 1976), p. 162.
2. John Newton quote from *Leaves of God, An Anthology of Prayers, Memorable Phrases, Inspirational Verse and Prose,*

Clyde Francis Lytle-ed. (Williamsport, PA: The Coslett Publishing Company, 1948), p. 13.

Chapter 17

1. Hans Selye quote from Harry Yoxall, *Retirement a Pleasure*, 1974.
2. Adaptation of Paul Evans and Fernando Bartolome material in Charles Handy, *Taking Stock, Being 50 in the 80s* (London: British Broadcasting Company), edited by Brigit Barry.

Other Good Harvest House Reading

HOW TO WIN OVER WORRY
by *John Haggai*

People need help in overcoming worry and need it desperately. The worry problem is at the root of much domestic strife, business failure, economic crises, incurable sicknesses, and premature deaths—to mention but a few of worry's hazards. Presenting more than a diagnosis, Dr. Haggai shows how God's Word offers the prescription for worry that can rid us of the devastating effects of worry forever.

HOW TO WIN OVER FEAR
by *John Haggai*

Fear is a pervasive and destructive influence in modern society. Everyone seems to be afraid of something. Dr. John Haggai explores the different types of fears, the essential prerequisites and formula for winning over fear, and God's power that is available to conquer fear. "You won't win over fear by reading this book or agreeing with it," says Dr. Haggai. "You have to do what it says."

HOW TO WIN OVER PAIN
by *John Haggai*

With the same clear insight and powerful answers that made *How to Win over Worry* a bestseller for more than 20 years, John Haggai now addresses the problem of pain in our lives. Covering the gamut from physical suffering to the emotional anguish of rejection, loneliness, death, or separation, *How to Win over Pain* asks the hard questions of life and presents God's strong and loving answers to our hurt and pain. Being equipped with biblical answers when pain strikes can help you be the victor instead of the victim of pain's devastating effects. Discover this powerful truth: God has fully provided everything needed to transform the pain in our lives into something powerful and good.

HOW TO WIN OVER LONELINESS
by *John Haggai*

With an engaging and encouraging openness about the circumstances that caused shyness to stalk him for years, author John Haggai shares his own encounter with loneliness. Without minimizing the power of circumstances in our lives, this internationally acclaimed author, lecturer, and founder of the Haggai Institute for Advanced Leadership Training presents two essential secrets that he and countless others have used to win victory over loneliness. Learn about the five lonely people: • The Sandgrain • The Outsider • The Lonely-in-Love • The Top Dog • The Ugly Duckling. Learn about the "blockouts" to overcoming loneliness, such as traveling and overeating. Learn to use the past as a resource. And learn about keeping our most important relationship intact—our relationship with God. A book that will spur readers to apply the truths and methods it presents.

IT TAKES SO LITTLE TO BE ABOVE AVERAGE
by *Florence Littauer*

"Nobody wants to be average, ordinary, dull, usual, run-of-the-mill! Then why do so many of us trudge down the middle lane of life and watch the years fly by?" Insights into human behavior which will greatly inspire you and enable you to rise above the norm.

REACHING YOUR FULL POTENTIAL
Establishing Goals in Your Life
by *Richard Furman, M.D.*

Reaching your full potential in any area of life can become a reality as you understand the importance of setting goals. Dr. Furman shares his story and the proven principles for turning dreams into reality.

LIVING WITHOUT LOSING
by *Don Polston*

Practical and to the point, this is the perfect handbook-devotional for the active Christian man or woman with a demanding schedule. Scripturally sound, practical insights on how to achieve success, peace of mind, increased energy, and much more.

WHERE WILL I FIND THE TIME?
Making Time Work For You
by *Sally McClung*

For most of us, the busier our lives become the less fulfilled we seem to be. *Where Will I find the Time?* offers realistic advice to everyone who wants to learn to use time more effectively. Once we learn the simple and basic principles for enjoying all the God-given dimensions of life, there's more than enough time to do the things that really matter.

Author Sally McClung shares her biblically-based insights for successfully prioritizing the demands of marriage, family, and work while still leaving opportunities for recreation and renewal. In her warm and personal style, the author provides encouragement to those who struggle with life management and personal organization skills and gives practical information that can increase your effectiveness without delay.

Dear Reader:

We would appreciate hearing from you regarding this Harvest House nonfiction book. It will enable us to continue to give you the best in Christian publishing.

1. What most influenced you to purchase *Be Careful What You Call Impossible*?
   - ☐ Author
   - ☐ Subject matter
   - ☐ Backcover copy
   - ☐ Recommendations
   - ☐ Cover/Title
   - ☐ _____

2. Where did you purchase this book?
   - ☐ Christian bookstore
   - ☐ General bookstore
   - ☐ Department store
   - ☐ Grocery store
   - ☐ Other

3. Your overall rating of this book:
   - ☐ Excellent ☐ Very good ☐ Good ☐ Fair ☐ Poor

4. How likely would you be to purchase other books by this author?
   - ☐ Very likely
   - ☐ Somewhat likely
   - ☐ Not very likely
   - ☐ Not at all

5. What types of books most interest you? (check all that apply)
   - ☐ Women's Books
   - ☐ Marriage Books
   - ☐ Current Issues
   - ☐ Self Help/Psychology
   - ☐ Bible Studies
   - ☐ Fiction
   - ☐ Biographies
   - ☐ Children's Books
   - ☐ Youth Books
   - ☐ Other _____

6. Please check the box next to your age group.
   - ☐ Under 18
   - ☐ 18-24
   - ☐ 25-34
   - ☐ 35-44
   - ☐ 45-54
   - ☐ 55 and over

Mail to: Editorial Director
Harvest House Publishers, Inc.
1075 Arrowsmith
Eugene, OR 97402

Name _____

Address _____

City _____ State _____ Zip _____

Thank you for helping us to help you in future publications!